ıl's Red Coat

HEA

Atticus

Will

Will's Red Coat

THE STORY OF ONE OLD DOG WHO
CHOSE TO LIVE AGAIN

Tom Ryan

piatkus

PIATKUS

First published in the United States in 2017 by HarperCollins
First published in Great Britain in 2017 by Piatkus
This paperback edition published in 2017 by Piatkus

A CIP catalogue record for this book
is available from the British Library.

ISBN 978-0-349-41187-3

Printed and bound in Great Britain by
Clays Ltd, St Ives plc

Papers used by Piatkus are from well-managed forests
and other responsible sources.

Piatkus
An imprint of
Little, Brown Book Group
Carmelite House
50 Victoria Embankment
London EC4Y 0DZ

An Hachette UK Company
www.hachette.co.uk

www.littlebrown.co.uk

To Ken and Ann Stampfer, whose love for the White Mountains is surpassed only by their love for each other.

After all, an animal is not just a thing with fur
    on it; it is a complete being.
—CARL JUNG, *Introduction to Jungian Psychology:*
    Notes of the Seminar on Analytical Psychology
    (1925)

He allowed himself to be swayed by his
    conviction that human beings are not born
    once and for all on the day their mothers give
    birth to them, but that life obliges them over
    and over again to give birth to themselves.
—GABRIEL GARCÍA MÁRQUEZ, *Love in the Time*
    of Cholera

Contents

The Forest

This is the forest primeval. The murmuring
   pines and the hemlocks,
Bearded with moss, and in garments green,
   indistinct in the twilight,
Stand like Druids of old . . .
   —HENRY WADSWORTH LONGFELLOW

I woke up early this morning. It was the rain. The way it was lashing at the window beside our bed and thundering down on the metal roof. A few degrees colder and all of this would be snow, and we'd be digging out all over again. As it is, the snow has finally melted from our yard, but plenty remains in the shady nooks of the forests and on the hillsides and summits. It is late April in the mountains of New Hampshire, where winter lingers and rivers run high, and the trout lilies and trillium have yet to appear. Waiting for spring here in the Mount Washington Valley can often feel like an act of faith.

It is still dark outside as I sit at my old scraped and scarred desk, a comfortable hand-me-down from a friend with an old Mississippi accent. A candle flickers, shadows sway, and the scent of cinnamon fills the room. A mug of tea sits next to the candle and a ribbon of steam rises before fading into the darkness. Atticus followed me out of bed earlier, but now he's sleeping again, this time on the bedding behind me on the floor. His snores speak of contentment, of the early hour, and of his age. Hanging on the wall above the desk is a map of the White Mountains. The two of us know nearly all of these peaks well and in every season. They are as familiar as old friends who wait for us just outside our back door and are as much our home as this cozy house is.

To the right, a tiny red coat with a thick white collar dangles from a hook. It looks a lot like Christmas and is just about the right size for an elf. There is a bit of magic in it. Of this I have no doubt. For that little coat gets me to stop many times each day to consider what matters in life and what it means to be human. That's why I didn't box it up and hide it away in the back of some closet. It is meant to be seen, because I don't ever want life to get so busy and complicated that I forget.

No, forgetting wouldn't do. Not that I ever could.

A favorite C. S. Lewis quote reminds us, "One day you will be old enough to read fairy tales again." Because of all I've seen and felt through the years, I've come to believe that if we are fortunate, we realize that we can also live them.

The mystery of new stories awaits each of us, something

that heartens me at the most difficult moments of my life. You could say that this is what I base my faith on. It is the belief that life goes on, no matter what. And no matter how long winter lingers, spring will always follow.

The memories clinging to that red jacket are not unlike the fairy tales my mother shared with me when I was very young and sitting on her lap, or the stories my father read to me after my mother died, as I lay in bed, too old for fairy tales. Stories of great adventures undertaken by improbable heroes. Those same whispers of possibilities reach out to remind me that many an incredible voyage began without warning. A wrong turn, an unlikely choice, a knock on the door, and the next thing you know, life is never the same. Sometimes even the grandest of stories are launched as regrets. They turn into an unforeseen voyage taking us from where we are to where we are supposed to be, and from who we are to who we are meant to be.

That coat hanging innocently from the hook is a reminder of the importance of letting go and leaping forward, of the depths of despair, the heights of love, and the bonds of friendship.

My goodness, that certainly is a heck of a lot for one tiny coat to carry.

Is it any wonder it is a talisman for me?

Sure, I have my memories and all those photographs, but this was his. And this is his story. Well . . . actually, it is our story. And maybe it wasn't the rain that woke me up, after all. Maybe it was simply time to tell it . . . to tell our fairy tale.

I am an introvert. It took fifty-four years for me to say it. Yes, I am a gregarious, chattering, emotionally expressive introvert. People who are just getting to know me don't understand that part. How is it that I'm not in the least bit shy, but I'm an introvert? They read my revealing words and see me with Atticus at book events talking and laughing freely in front of hundreds of people, and they don't get it. I don't blame them. I didn't get it myself until recently.

It feels good to come clean, to know myself. When I finally admitted it, I felt like I was on the first of twelve steps. But with introversion, there's only one step. You recognize yourself. What follows is peace and empowerment. You no longer have to try to fit in. You finally understand your social anxiety, and why you are allergic to shallow conversation. But I warn you, don't get me started on anything I'm passionate about, like my favorite hiking trails in the White Mountains; the Boston Red Sox outfield of Betts, Bradley, and Benintendi; watermelon; or the latest volume of Mary Oliver poetry. You won't be able to shut me up.

I can also go days without speaking a word and feel the freedom in that extended silence. Words are as essential to me as oxygen, sleep, food, and water. But I don't need to prattle on endlessly like I used to, in order to revel in their glory. I can read, or write letters to friends, or write my newspaper column and blog posts. Words are prayers, spoken or silently ruminated.

How, after five decades, did I discover I was an introvert? Easy. It's the way I've discovered many truths about life. The forest told me.

Don't forget, this is a fairy tale, and no fairy tale seems quite right without an enchanted forest. It just so happens that we live on the edge of one.

When people ask me where Jackson, New Hampshire, is,

I tell them it is halfway to wild. Ten miles to the south is the bustling ski and vacation town of North Conway, with its outlet stores. Ten miles to the north is one of the wildest, fiercest weather outposts in the world—the summit of Mount Washington. Although I prefer Agiocochook, the name the Abenaki gave that sacred peak: the home of the Great Spirit.

But who am I kidding? We aren't just halfway to wild; wild is right outside our door. We walk down the stairs and cross the yard to the bear path that descends beyond the high grass into the tall trees and ferns until we get to the river. We rock-hop to the other side and we're in a magic realm. Within minutes we enter the White Mountain National Forest, a place the size of the state of Rhode Island. Trails spider-web out from there for over a thousand miles. We visit with wild things as often as possible, and occasionally wild things spill out of the forest, across the river, and up into our backyard as well. You see, wild goes both ways.

Here on the edge of enchantment, I have learned to be quiet. I can sit and listen to the river's flow, the chatter of crows, the night songs of owls, and the wind sighing through the birch leaves. I've learned to accept the seasons of the year, and those that make up a lifetime.

I laugh more, talk less, and don't always answer the phone. I read whenever I can and cozy up with one poem at a time, always in search of sublime sentences that stir things in me I may never completely understand. I gave my television away, but music is always playing. Music and laughter abide in this little home—and quiet, of course.

Often it's Billie Holiday or Louis Armstrong who fills these four rooms with rhythm and soul and provides the soundtrack to our day. I also enjoy streaming WCRB, a classical station out of Boston, particularly when I'm writing or when I'm in a pensive mood.

While not a religious man, I say my prayers more than I ever have, and not just at night. Since I never learned many of the prayers I was supposed to when I was an altar boy, I make up my own as I go. They are more like conversations with God, who plays the role of a friend who is a good listener. In my most common prayer, I list what I'm grateful for, and starting out each day like this reminds me what I have instead of what I don't. Sometimes my gratitude is for grand things like my life or health or friendships. At other times, it can be for something as silly or ordinary as a new toothbrush, or being thankful that I don't use an alarm clock.

Then again, I don't need an alarm clock, thanks to the three crows who gather in the black ash tree right outside our bedroom window. They define the word "cacophony" for me whenever I hear their racket, as they caw and squawk and shriek at one another. But some days I get the impression that they're actually cawing and squawking and shrieking at me, in the hope that I will get out of bed and overfill the bird feeder or leave bread crumbs scattered about as I do in the winter.

For most of my life I didn't understand the music of the forest, and I was afraid of the song. That's when my friend Atticus came along and everything changed. He was only eight weeks old the first time we went into the woods in the western edge of Newburyport, Massachusetts. I had just said good-bye to Maxwell Garrison Gillis, an elderly dog who made his home with me for the last year and a half of his life. His time with me led me to care for someone other than myself, or the city I was obsessively reporting on in my small newspaper, the *Undertoad*.

Before Max, there was little more than meetings and politics in my life—and heroes and villains, and above all, stress. One only had to look at his middle and last name to understand how important my small city life was to me. I'd given Max the middle name of Garrison, after William Lloyd Garrison, the great liberator who was at the crux of the fight for emancipation. He was a son of Newburyport, as was Andrew J. "Bossy" Gillis, the former bad-boy mayor who was infamous at the same time as Boston's James Michael Curley and New York's Jimmy Walker. Both Garrison and Gillis were considered troublemakers who published muckraking newspapers, as was I.

After Max, there was Atticus Maxwell Finch.

I wanted Atticus to experience things Max had never known, at least not that I knew of. Max came to me with a truckload of emotional baggage, and when I held him in my arms as life left him, he left with my heart. Atticus brought it back to me, but more than that, his job was to live a life so full that he'd make up for the one Max had missed out on before I met him.

From the beginning I treated Atticus as a peer, not a pet. While society wanted him to be my baby or my son, and for me to be his pet parent or fur dad, from the beginning we were simply Tom and Atticus. I used polite requests instead of commands, and words like "please" and "thank you" were of the utmost importance to me.

"Atticus, would you have a seat, please. Thank you."

I talked to him and treated him as my equal—for he was. There was no need for words like "master" or "owner." No need for a collar or a leash—not after the first couple of years, anyway, when he could safely make his way throughout the world with me. Atticus was brought up to be unapologetically himself. My goal was to protect him from the limitations of society and to allow him to thrive. I wanted him to experience everything life had to offer. That's where the forest came in.

Max was a beach dog. He frolicked on Plum Island each morning and evening. Other than that, he was on leash as I crisscrossed downtown Newburyport chasing after the latest stories about misbehaving police officers, lying city officials, and greedy developers. Oh, don't get me wrong, I also wrote about good folk. Heroes *and* villains, remember?

Max had a good life with me. But I wanted so much more for him. Unfortunately, there was nothing I could do about that. Therefore, I did the next best thing and used his short time with me as my inspiration in giving Atticus more . . . more of everything.

I suppose that wasn't the only factor in raising Atticus as I did. I'd had my own oppressive upbringing as the youngest of Jack and Isabel Ryan's nine children, and perhaps this inspired me as much as my regrets about Max. No matter what the reason, I wanted Atticus to have the freedom and the unconditional love that Max, and I, had gone without.

Atticus was a miniature Schnauzer, just as Max was. Originally I made the mistake of wanting another Max, but there was only ever the one. And hence I was off on a great learning curve. Even writing the name of a breed makes me feel uncomfortable these days; the older I get, the more I reject labels and limitations. I don't like to judge a species, a breed, a nationality, or a creed. My preference is to seek out what connects instead of what divides. While I fully understood that Atticus was a dog, I'd never treated him or limited him as one, except when it came to his physical needs. He was always simply Atticus.

Atticus and I went to the forest for the scents and the wildlife. In those earliest of days, wildlife was blue jays and gray squirrels. Young Atticus would give chase, and I'd whisper in his ear, "Be gentle, please. They have as much right to be here as you do."

Everything in the world was new to eight-week-old Atticus, but he became especially animated in the forest, where the fragrances, the sounds, and the textures greeted him. The forest was also somewhat new to me, and it was a return to my greatest fear.

I was seven when my mother died. Isabel Ryan dropped a lit cigarette on her hospital bed and died of burn complications six days before Christmas. Before that, the mother I knew had multiple sclerosis. She wore braces on her legs and moved about the house on metal crutches that wrapped around her forearms, and out in the world in a wheelchair. I don't remember much about her. There are not many photographs, and we don't have the kind of family that plumbs the depths of intimacy.

My father, Jack Ryan, worked hard to provide for us, and we were relieved when he was working because of his unpredictable, seething temper. The belt, a backhand, or crushing words were delivered to us without much warning. He was a volcano, always on the edge of erupting, and we were like some primitive tribe that deified him as we feared him.

In those first years after my mother died, I used to walk with some of my older brothers to the end of the lane. There was an old farmhouse where an ancient farmer and his wife lived. I rarely saw them and don't remember them ever talking. Then again, I don't remember much about those years. They are gone. I think I misplaced them on purpose, perhaps to protect that seven-year-old who hurt too much.

What I *do* remember is that tangle of forgotten field beyond the farmhouse, and the way it swept slightly downhill to a sprinkling of trees that grew into a dark and ominous forest. It both fascinated and frightened me. It was so dense, it was more shadow than light, more night than day. Strange sounds would greet us, birds and animals and other things I'd never see. On windy days the trees would moan and groan. Boulders would appear as sleeping beasts. The entire place felt as if it were one enormous monster and we were walking in its belly. I'd hurry along to make sure I wasn't the last in line. We'd walk down, down, down into the sylvan netherworld until we came to a river. There the sun pierced the darkness and the song of the water over the stones was enchantment itself. It was an ethereal melody, bittersweet to my young heart. I'd hear whispers from the water, and from the leaves stirring in the breeze above, and from the deepest shadows and small caves. "Come closer," it hissed. "Come closer."

Another voice, this one from within, urged me, "Run! Run home!"

On the nights after we visited those eerie woods, I'd have nightmares. My father would wake me and say it was just a dream, but the dream was all too real. It would return again and again. I'd fall asleep, after pulling my covers over my head, leaving just enough of a hole for my nose to breathe through. When I tumbled into slumber, I'd hear the voices again: "Come closer . . . closer."

"Run away!" cried the other voice. "Run fast. Run now."

In my dreams the trees by the river would pull up their roots and menacingly march up the hill, across that tangle of field by the sleeping farmer and his wife, and they'd gather outside my bedroom window.

"Come closer."

The forest called to me. Always.

One day when I was home alone the siren song reached out to me, and I followed it. I stopped at the edge of the field, in the last light I'd see for a while. I looked behind me and wanted to turn back, but something pulled me deeper and I surrendered. Across rocks and roots, through shadows, beyond columns of pine trees that felt as if they were watching me, I walked as if spellbound. Down, down to the river I went, where the fairy song was the loudest, and the stillness of the woods pushed me forward to the current.

"Come closer. Come closer."

"Run away!"

I grew drowsy looking at the river's glint and glimmer as it flowed by me. I swayed in place—waiting, waiting, waiting, for *what* I didn't know. But it felt natural, and it felt unnatural.

I feared I would be taken, as in the refrain from Yeats's "The Stolen Child":

> Come away, O human child!
> To the waters and the wild
> With a faery, hand in hand,
> For the world's more full of weeping
> than you can understand.

That's when I ran. I ran as fast and as hard as I could, tripping and falling, stumbling to my feet again, breathless, wheezing for air, not getting any, my heart racing, my lungs screaming. I hopped over dead trees, past ferns that grabbed at my ankles, beyond the shadows and the gloom, and away from the ever-present, ever-louder words, "Come closer!"

I raced through the last tunnel of trees toward the field, and when I made it, I fell to my knees to drink in the air. I didn't dare stay there for too long. I was afraid of what I imagined as an enormous unholy hand reaching out, pulling me back into the despair, never to be heard from again.

That was my last time in that darkest of places, from the darkest moment of my young life. I believed if I returned, I wouldn't find my way home. I would be lost forever, and forgotten, just as I was already forgetting my mother—what she looked like, her voice when she spoke to me, the smell of her red lipstick when she read to me on her lap.

We were all lost in those years after my mother died. My father, who used to beat us, didn't as much anymore. The violence waned, but his temper didn't. He grew tired and sullen. With each passing year it was worse. When I was in high school, and the last one in the house with him, it had become a silent, stifling place, and I was a sulking, moody teen. I came to think of him as a man who was tired of living.

My childhood was defined by loss—Isabel dying, Jack decomposing, brothers and sisters fleeing. Whatever innocence I had shriveled up and died. Even hope was impossible to come by. I felt a kinship to D. H. Lawrence the moment I read: "If I think of my childhood it is always as if there was a sort of inner darkness . . ."

Into my twenties, thirties, and even early forties, I'd fall asleep and be visited by that chilling song of the trees and the river, "Come closer. Come closer."

I did just the opposite. I avoided woodlands and sought out the safety of civil places. As I grew up, and grew older, I'd find comfort in bustling communities and a distracted life. I didn't want quiet, because quiet meant I was inviting the song to reach out to me again. Even then, it would always come, usually when I was sleeping and defenseless.

However, in my attempt to stay safe, I was also half dead.

I became brave only for tiny Atticus, bringing him to Moseley Pines in Newburyport, where he could experience what he needed. He immediately felt at home there, and I discovered that strangely so did I. Hours were spent in a glade of lady slippers, my back to a tree, while I read and Atticus sat up watching the breath of the forest. The way it sighed and settled, how it welcomed shafts of sunlight, and mists that wove like ghosts on chill days when the rains had stopped, or how in winter, the snow among the pines turned it into the holiest cathedral I'd ever been in. Those brief excursions across town led to weekends away in the pastoral hills of Vermont, which led to short hikes and grew into longer walks, which brought us eventually to the mountains of New Hampshire. There we became nemophilists, haunters of woods.

Two years and hundreds of mountains climbed later, I sold the *Undertoad* and moved north with Atticus. Thousands of mountains later, *Following Atticus* was published. It detailed the experiences of two unlikely novice hikers: a dog who was considered too small, and an overweight newspaper editor who had a fear of heights.

I started a Facebook page, for marketing purposes, and the page brought readers. They were captivated by the photos I shared of Atticus in breathtaking scenes, or sitting serenely and Buddha-like on summits throughout this glorious enchanted forest. The more I shared, the more was shared with me. Those who were following me while I followed Atticus started sharing stories about their own fears, triumphs, and travails.

Yes, the forest that had always called to me, had always wanted me to come closer, was welcoming me home at last, by way of Atticus, and his primitive and peaceful heart.

My aunt Marijane Ryan, my father's youngest sister and a former nun who had left the Church to become a therapist and who worked in hospice, pointed out that Jung thought of the forest as a place of the unknown in us. It is frightening, and eventually can turn into a place of transformation or of refuge, depending upon where you are in your personal journey.

It had been all three to me, and now the forest is my refuge.

The mythologist Joseph Campbell, whose life's work was the monomyth, also known as the hero's journey, knew a great deal about Jung as well, and his lectures and books often echoed him. In *A Joseph Campbell Companion: Reflections on the Art of Living*, Campbell said, "It is by going down into the abyss that we recover the treasures of life . . . The very cave you are afraid to enter turns out to be the source of what you are looking for. The damn thing in the cave that was dreaded has become the center."

On my hero's journey, I was guided by Atticus, who was not at all human and perhaps not all animal either. He fell somewhere in between, it seemed to me. By following him, I found peace in my life.

Then the universe conspired to change our lives again. It's how *he* showed up and turned our peaceful world upside down. But it began innocently enough. The forest had helped me, and I thought it would help another lost soul as well.

I t began as many a beginning does, with an end.

His name was William then. He was fifteen. He couldn't see very well. He couldn't hear at all. His body ached with neglect and the torment of the years. Age had not been kind to him and fate had cast him adrift. I'm told that the only people he had ever lived with had grown too old to take care of themselves, and it would become clear to me that they hadn't taken care of William for a long time either. Ultimately, he was left at a kill shelter in New Jersey.

Whenever I think of this part, and I think of it often, I imagine how that had to feel for him. How hopeless and cold. How empty. How haunted he had to be that first night all alone. I think of the smells of disinfectant, urine, feces, and fear, with fear being the worst. I think of his confusion, and how he could see little and hear nothing. I imagined his underfed body shivering, because that's what he did when he showed up in our lives a few days later.

As providence would have it, he was removed from that shelter by an organization called New Jersey Schnauzer Rescue when a volunteer contacted the group about William's plight. That's when I heard about him.

A lone photograph of William and a paragraph or two were posted on the New Jersey Schnauzer Rescue Facebook page. They wrote that his was one of the saddest cases they had ever seen. It was shared, with social media spreading the post across the world. Eventually, our friend Laura Bachofner shared it on the *Following Atticus* Facebook page, which was growing in popularity since our book had been published eight months earlier. She hoped one of our six thousand fans might take William in.

Atticus and I were sitting on the couch the night I noticed the post, which featured a photo of William looking shaggy and perhaps a bit hot. His tongue was hanging out of his mouth, and his ghostly eyes gave evidence of cataracts. I wished him well. I'd check back every now and then to watch the responses. Many wrote about how sad it was that he was given up at his age. Some were livid about it. Others wrote that they would take him, but . . . There were a lot of reasons listed, but they all translated to one thing: William was probably not going to find a home. That's when I did a most unexpected thing, and William's destiny took yet another unforeseen turn.

I wrote that Atticus and I would take him.

When I sent out an e-mail to our friends informing them we were bringing old William to live with us, I don't think anyone believed me. It had always been just Atticus and me, with the occasional girlfriend here and there. For the ten years we had been together, I'd never had a desire for much more, and I had no reason to believe Atticus felt any differently. He'd never been fond of other dogs. He liked greeting them, but within seconds he would move on. It had always been this way. Perhaps it had to do with him being the only one in his litter, a discovery that surprised his breeder, Paige Foster. She had expected at least two other pups and had never been wrong about that kind of thing. Years later she would tell me that this was her first sign that Atticus was different.

My friend Cheryl was the first to respond to my e-mail, warning me against bringing William home. "Don't do it, Tom. That little guy is at the end of his life, and nothing but blindness, incontinence, and cancer are ahead for him. It will be all stress and heartache. There will be expensive vet bills and then he'll die. You and Atticus don't need that sadness, and that's all there will be."

Another friend offered similar advice over lunch. I asked him, "What would you do if the situation was reversed?"

"I told you," he said. "I wouldn't take him. It's not worth it. You and Atti have a great life. Your first book just came out. You're on top of the world. Why change it?"

"No. I meant what would you have me do if you were the one who was old, in pain, alone, and had no place to call home?"

My friends were well intentioned, but I wasn't asking their advice.

My mind was made up. It was as simple as William needing a home and the slim prospects of him finding one. It was like a switch had flipped, and that was that. But isn't that how so many of life's most important decisions are made? A flash of awakening, a jolt of acknowledgment, a decision made—no matter how unrealistic it may seem. At least that's how the most influential choices I've made have come about. Passion had more to do with them than reason did. My head doesn't stand a chance when my heart leads the way. I've nearly always trusted my intuition, and when I haven't, things haven't gone as well.

Sometimes you don't understand what you do until long after you've done it. But right then, while it was unfolding, I was inexorably drawn to have him here. Two thoughts came to mind. First, no one should have to die alone. And I asked myself, *What would I wish for Atticus if something happened to me, and he was without a home and was just as frightened and confused?*

If I gave it thought beyond that, it was envisioning a simple transition to life with a kindly dog. I imagined the refreshing mountain air infusing him with peace and giving him some enjoyment at the end of his life. Maybe we could get him up a short peak along an easy trail, even if I had to carry him up in a backpack. And, of course, I felt the forest would help as it reached across the river up to our home.

Five days later we met William for the first time. It was in a hotel parking lot in Connecticut. Three members of the New Jersey Schnauzer Rescue group were with him. They were excited to meet Atticus because they'd read our book, and to them, as fans of the breed, he was a celebrity. They were elated when he greeted each of them, and when I saw William . . .

My God, when I saw William, I was horrified.

My insides were churning, and I was wondering how he was still living, why he was still living. I felt sick, thinking it was cruel that someone had kept him alive. There was nothing to him. He was as brittle as a leftover husk the winter winds had hollowed out.

William was white except for dark feathering on top of his nose and at the tips of his pointed ears. He had long black eyelashes that would later become a focal point of his face, but I didn't notice them that first day. I was concentrating on the way he walked. The lack of flexibility in his joints made each step a painful one. His spine was rigid and appeared to be the source of a catch in each step. His straight front legs reached out, but his hind legs held him back, which led to an almost lyrical gait, almost like a rocking horse. He was underweight to the point of being bony. Someone had given him a rough haircut since I'd seen his photograph, but it only accentuated how fragile he was.

I greeted him with treats, offering them to both Atticus and William at the same time. Atticus gently took his from between my fingertips, one at a time, while William lunged roughly at my other hand as he hunted for the snacks, nipping at my fingers. I would later understand that this had to do mostly with his poor eyesight. I had no doubt that the volunteers had taken wonderful care of him in the few days before delivering him to us, but he didn't seem confident of when he'd see his next meal.

We said our good-byes to the three volunteers and I asked Atticus if he would like to hop into the backseat. He complied, although he had always sat up front next to me. I put William in the front passenger seat so I could watch him. When I lifted William, he turned wild, snapping and snarling and whipping his head around trying to bite me. It was so sudden and such a shock that I nearly dropped him.

The man in the group offered an apologetic smile and said, "Yeah, he does that. It helps if you have one hand on the back of his collar so he can't get at you."

I hadn't done a lot of homework on William, but I'd been told two things that made me feel comfortable about bringing him home:

"He's very sweet."

"He gets along well with other dogs."

It was only when we entered Massachusetts heading north that I realized Atticus hadn't interacted with William.

We stopped twice for William to go to the bathroom before we reached New Hampshire. Each time he thrashed around in my arms, with teeth snapping and high-pitched yips and yelps.

I wanted to throw up.

M ax had been an older dog when I took him in. I never quite knew his age, but he was believed to be between twelve and fourteen. Like William, I gave him a home without giving it much thought when I feared he wouldn't find another place to live.

When I first met Max, he was at a groomer. She'd given him a bath, and he was waiting for me.

When I showed up, she wasn't anywhere to be found.

When the groomer appeared, she showed me a little dog who looked more like a sheep. He was all gray hair—a bushel of it—with a black nose and chestnut-brown eyes that could barely be seen under a thick curtain of eyebrows.

I wasn't sure what to make of him. But he was kind, and while I didn't have a leash or collar with me, I didn't need one. He followed me out the door happily, hopping into the front passenger seat of the car, and that was that. We were together. I was his, and he was mine.

During our first few weeks, he'd bark nonstop in my third-floor apartment whenever I left him alone. Eventually, that would cease, and Maxwell Garrison Gillis became a perfect roommate. It was all very easy.

A dozen years later, as Atticus and I were driving north with William, my anger simmered, and I considered calling back the rescue group and telling them, "We're bringing him back. You can keep the check, but this dog is suffering."

I tried to call Christine O'Connell, our veterinarian at North Country Animal Hospital, from one of the rest areas, but I couldn't reach her. I think it was mostly to vent, but I also wanted to let her know that we might have to make an extremely tough decision about his life.

I drove in brooding silence after that. Atticus sat in the back watching the scenery fly by the windows. When I looked at William, lying just a foot away with his eyes closed, my friend Cheryl's advice echoed in my ears: "Don't do it, Tom. There'll be nothing but stress and heartache."

I'm not sure why I didn't call the rescue folks. Goodness

knows I wanted to. I even made a deal with myself that if I called before reaching the mountains, it would somehow be okay to return him, but if he made it to the beaver pond at the foot of Mount Moosilauke, I'd keep him. I kept telling myself to call. *Call. Don't put it off.* And yet I drove on in a daze, chewing my lip, stewing about what to do.

Back and forth I went, reaching for the phone, putting it down. All the while I grew increasingly upset. We had just met him, and I was thinking about putting him out of his misery. It shouldn't have come to this. The responsibility of that choice shouldn't have fallen to me.

When we reached the beaver pond in Kinsman Notch, we had entered into the White Mountains and the decision was made. There was no turning back; William was our responsibility. When we pulled into a rest area, he tried to bite me again.

He walked around the parking lot and then into the water. I looked at his stiff spine, and how fragile he was, and the way he seemed lost. I wondered if he even knew he was now standing in the pond.

Atticus watched all of this, and I looked over at him.

"I think I screwed up, my friend."

He just looked at me. Who knows what he was thinking? But seeing his gentle face, that intent gaze, I promised myself that I would never let Atticus suffer as William was. I would see to it that he would never be in such pain.

In Lincoln, an hour from home, we stopped one last time, and this was when William's teeth finally found their mark. He caught my thumb in his mouth and bit down. I tried to jerk away, but his bite tightened. I felt him pierce my skin and go deep. Blood trickled down my thumb.

My initial instinct was to strike out, to take my free hand and knock him away. I could never imagine hitting Maxwell or Atticus, but they had never attacked me like that.

My hand reared back and I readied myself to backhand him—but then I stopped.

Something else took hold, something stronger than the burning pain in my hand and my rage. It was instantaneous and involuntary.

Call it an epiphany of sorts, if you will. Or heavenly intervention. Or something else beyond my ability to comprehend.

With my hand tensed to strike, I stopped thinking about the William I was expecting to meet and instead put myself in his place. I thought about what had been done to him. He had had no say in what had befallen him, no say about the pain in his body, about being betrayed, about being left alone in a strange place, about being passed from stranger to stranger.

I took a deep breath. I took another.

Slowly my anger eased.

I took another breath.

I let him have my thumb. I took my free hand and placed it on his head, speaking softly to ears that couldn't hear me.

"I know you are afraid and feeling betrayed, and you are in pain. I guess I'd be just as angry and probably act the same way. I'm sorry. I'm sorry for everything."

When he felt my hand stroking the feathery white hair on top of his head, he bit down harder. I winced, swallowed hard, and swore.

"I'll help you any way I can. I'll help you get to where you need to be, no matter where that is. I don't want you to be in any more pain. I promise, William."

He held tight to my thumb until it seemed more his than

mine. Blood flowed and my palm was streaked with red. When he finally relaxed, I pulled free.

Shaken, I got back into the car, sitting next to this dog who had bitten me. Sadness and regret filled me, and I understood that I'd have to live with this horrible mistake.

I washed out the wound with water and hand sanitizer. I wrapped a Band-Aid around it; then, because it was still bleeding, I put a larger one over the first.

When we arrived home, I had to carry William up to our second-floor apartment. He twisted in my arms and yelped again and again, with his teeth snapping as I held him away from my body and tried not to drop him. When I placed him on the living room floor, he reared up on his hind legs, high-pitched barks coming out in rapid fire like a machine gun, his teeth coming at me as he twisted violently and out of control, finally falling over on his side.

Atticus quickly hopped to safety in his usual spot on the couch, which was too high for William. William fought but failed to get back on his feet. He writhed helplessly on the floor. I sat on the other end of the couch with my legs folded and my feet beneath me, also out of reach. Atticus watched and listened to William, and then looked to me. I dropped my head into my hands and wished I could turn the clock back five days.

None of the three of us had any reason to be happy on our first day together.

For a decade, Atticus and I had spoiled each other. There were the regular growing pains a puppy goes through while figuring out his place in the world, but nothing significant. Most of those troubles had to do with housetraining.

Otherwise it was a seamless relationship, no matter what life threw at us. We moved in sync with each other, and we regularly communicated through our expressions and the smallest of gestures. Me giving a nod to let him know something was okay, or tossing my head to one side as if to say *let's go*. He, lifting his floppy ears to say yes and lowering them to say no, or shaking his head to express his displeasure. Certain looks say just enough between fast friends. The understanding is complete.

It didn't take long for ours to become a leashless and mostly wordless life where two were becoming one. Whenever anyone asked how I did it, how I got Atticus to be that way, I'd tell them, "We just hang out together."

Still, they were amazed at how well we went about our lives together, but what we were doing was nothing new. It's the way our two species have learned from each other for thousands of years. It wasn't until dogs became pets and accessories that a sacrosanct bond was diluted, and changed for a busier and more distracted way of life.

There was only one time when Atticus went to the bathroom in our home after the initial puppy stage. We were still living in Newburyport and Atticus had eaten something that didn't agree with him. I woke up the next morning to the stench of diarrhea. I wasn't mad. However, I had him sit with me while I cleaned it up. It's something I did with him as a puppy too, and even though I spoke to him calmly, his ears sagged while he ducked his head. His diarrhea continued throughout the day, but we were outside so often that it wasn't a problem. When we hopped into bed that night, I called him over and said, "If you have to go to the bathroom tonight, please wake me up and I'll take you outside."

I was awakened by a nudge of his nose against my chin at two in the morning. Strange and curious Atticus was letting me know he had to go out.

There have been other nights when Atticus has awakened me for similar reasons, but there was never another accident in our home in those ten years.

Atticus never barked, although about a half-dozen times a year he'd see a friend of ours approaching and let out a howl of happiness. He also did this occasionally when we walked into a bank or a store that offered him treats. Now and then this silent fellow let out a great exclamation announcing his arrival. Mostly, though, there wasn't a peep from him.

He would never misbehave. I could leave my food within his reach and he wouldn't touch it even if I was out of the room. And he wouldn't go into the trash.

Our friends often refer to Atticus as either dignified or thoughtful. I think both work.

The first time she met him, Laura Bachofner tried to hug Atticus, and he gave her a look she describes as "not in a thousand years." She stopped trying and referred to him as a snob. But once she got to know him better, she agreed with the "dignified" description.

The first morning we woke up to life with William in it, there was a puddle in the hallway. Atticus reached it first and stopped in midstride, holding a foot above it. He looked back at me, his eyes wide, his ears low, and he retreated. I cleaned it up, and only then would he pass. But as he did, he crouched and seemed to hurry, as if the floor were contaminated.

When I took him out, William continued to thrash about while I carried him down the stairs. He grew calm when I put him on the grass in the backyard and stayed calm when

I picked him back up. But he flew into his fit of anger when I put him on the floor again. It would become a routine for him; carrying him down the stairs was fine, but not up them.

Whenever he was angry after being carried up the stairs, he reminded me of a drunken leprechaun who wanted to fight. Almost always he'd lose his balance and topple over. His fury would continue for a little while he thrashed on the floor, and then his old age would take over and he'd fall asleep right where he was.

William's need to sleep was my ally, for I could count on him to nap most of the day away. But unlike Atticus and Maxwell before him, when I looked at him sleeping, I didn't see peace. Even as he slumbered, he looked troubled. Maybe it was just his body, the way it was so broken looking, or maybe it was because I knew he was depressed and lonely and wanted little to do with us.

There were days I'd walk Atticus while William was sleeping, and when we returned home I'd see his eyes open, but he wouldn't acknowledge us. Within a week of being in Jackson, he'd start sleeping in the bedroom during the day, and he'd hide away from us when we were home.

I don't doubt that Atticus was relieved that William rarely approached him; I could tell by the rise and fall of his ears. And Atticus wouldn't approach William. Then again, Atticus has never seemed to understand anger in others. He was befuddled whenever we encountered aggressive dogs. Watching William's temper tantrums upset him and made it seem unlikely there would be a friendship between the two of them. And if it weren't for that reason, it would have been because of William's bathroom habits.

William didn't care where he urinated or defecated. I

think it was more than just old age and his inability to hold it. He was unfazed by the daily messes he left around the house, and there was nothing I could do about it, since William was deaf and had diminished vision and hated being redirected.

On one of his first few days, I brought him outside. Twenty minutes later we were back inside and he stood looking at me, then squatted, leaving a pile of excrement in the middle of the floor. There was no shame or embarrassment. Atticus left the room in a hurry, but William simply sauntered around with his little up-and-down broken gait, until he came upon me cleaning it up. When he drew close, he watched me. He was very nonchalant about piss and shit.

Atticus was also bothered by how William walked into the water bowl and spilled the contents, leaving the ceramic dish clattering on the floor. Or how he'd knock things over that were in the way, such as a broom that would slap loudly when it fell. Or how he'd walk into the narrow space between the toilet and the wall, or the bathroom sink and the wall, or under the kitchen table and chairs, and get stuck, unable to back up. I'd hear a whimper, but it would soon turn into shrieks of frustration and then panic. Atticus would come and get me if I wasn't in the room, and I would carefully set William free, as if I were defusing a bomb, for his frustration was always directed at me.

Because William slept so much during the day, he often wandered at night. I'd wake up to his cries if he went to the bathroom on the wooden floor and fell in it. He was unable to get a grip to get up, and the more he struggled, the more he smeared feces and urine on his white coat.

This is when I felt the worst for him—to see him helpless like that, an obviously proud fellow, stuck on the floor in his mess. He'd whimper. He'd cry. If I managed to sleep through all of that, eventually I would hear almost human shrieks coming from him. And even when I helped him up, he'd lunge at me, teeth bared.

One night, I awakened to William's wails. I found him in a pile of feces, helpless and stinking. I ran warm water for the tub, and when I picked him up, I wasn't careful enough. He grabbed hold of my long sleeve and the forearm below it, and he bit down. I cursed and tried to pull him off, but he wouldn't budge, and the more I pulled at him with my free arm, the harder he bit me. Finally, I shook my arm, and he fell with a thud. He lay crying and whimpering, and I feared that he'd broken something. His ancient body was only bruised, but something else had broken when I heard him wail. It was my heart.

I hated William's attacks. I was disgusted by the way he made our home stink. And I often regretted taking him in because of how it was affecting Atticus. And yet there was something about him that made my heart ache.

What had this world done to him?

Was it only neglect? Or was it also abuse? I'll never know, and I'm not sure it matters. Both are sins against the living. My job was to pick up the pieces of his broken life and try to figure out what to do next.

I tried to be compassionate, but there were many days William and I were evenly matched, because he didn't like me and I didn't like him. And that was only in the first week or two. Publicly, I painted a happy scene, but my friends and our vet, Christine O'Connell, would hear my exasperation. I constantly thought about giving up, but always remembered how I'd given William my word that first day.

As I sit here tonight typing away, Copland's *Appalachian Spring* is playing, and in the soft glow of the desk lamp I see the scars on my hands. I call them "William scars." How many times he drew blood. How many times he made me curse him, and whatever made him that way; and how I wondered what I'd done by bringing him here. How many times I had to contain my temper as his teeth broke my skin and left my flesh burning like it was on fire.

Cheryl called to check in one day when things were at their worst and to say "I told you so."

"Are you seeing anything positive out of bringing William home, Tom? Anything at all?"

"You know how much I swear. More than most, right?"

"Definitely!"

"If there is a positive, I think William is helping me become more creative with my swearing."

I thought continually about Cheryl's words in those first weeks: "There'll be nothing but stress and heartache."

William wouldn't bite me every day, but he tried. Sometimes it was because he'd tip over the trash in the kitchen and I'd pull him away. He'd lunge again and again at me until I had to put the bin between us as a shield. The second time it happened I reached for the broom and took advantage of his weak back legs, sweeping a snarling, maniacal William away, much to his frustration and my relief. It felt like a victory as I exclaimed, "Ha! Take that, you son of . . ."

Fifteen minutes later, when I sat on the couch, he stood on the other side of the coffee table glaring at me. Like a broken old man, he struggled to pull himself up to a standing position, slowly stretching the kinks out of his body. When he was at his full height, his front paws on the table, he worked his way around the edge toward me, shrill barks filling the air. He was like a demon in some horror movie.

I laughed when I left the couch and stood behind the broom in the kitchen again while Atticus sat watching the scene, his ears drooping. I wasn't thinking of Cheryl's words then, but of what the volunteers from New Jersey Schnauzer Rescue had reported.

He's very sweet, my ass.

In defense of the folks from the rescue, they barely knew him. He was quickly passed from one to another in the few days they had him. Even in their politically correct way, when they wrote about the day we met in a *Huffington Post* piece, they referred to William as "cantankerous."

I wouldn't have minded a cantankerous William, I don't think. What I had an issue with was his aggressiveness toward me.

D uring William's first days there were errands to run, and out in public he lost his edge toward me. He'd allow me to place him in his nest of blankets on the floor of the back-seat of the car without incident. When we went to Four Your Paws Only to have him fitted for a harness, he wasn't leaping for joy about hanging out with his best friend, but he was patient, and he seemed to at least accept that I was on his side.

On the second day, Atticus and I dropped him off with Tracy at the Ultimutt Cut Pet Salon. If I hadn't know bet-ter, I would have thought he hated my leaving him there. He hadn't used the crate I had bought for him in the two nights he'd stayed with us, and when Tracy placed him in one, he became enraged, so she let him roam around the salon while she worked on other dogs.

When Atticus and I returned to pick him up, William was relieved to see us again. I could tell by the way he accepted me pulling him close and yielded into my chest. Tracy hadn't been so lucky; he'd tried to bite her several times when she groomed him.

On the third day, he met our veterinarian, Christine O'Connell, when she examined him. I told her how he was disrupting the tranquility of our home, and I admitted I was ambivalent about him. William definitely wasn't the sweet old fellow I'd heard about, and with each day I was increasingly regretting my decision.

Christine looked at his eyes and talked about his cataracts. They weren't complete, and she believed he could make out shapes and sizes and some detail, but not a lot. He obviously already recognized me, and he looked at her when she was talking about him and asking me questions.

He was completely deaf. His teeth were rotting. She wondered if William had ever had a cleaning done, and some of his teeth needed to come out. His gums were a mess, both green and black in places. They were receding to the point where the roots of some of his teeth were showing.

When Christine put William through range-of-motion exercises, she discovered something telling about him. I had assumed his faulty hips were due to arthritis, but she didn't detect any signs of it. One of the vet techs suggested that William's stiffness was due to lack of exercise. She talked about how in a former job she had encountered others that had similar issues with their hips. It was suggested that William had been confined to a small space, such as a crate, for far too long. This made sense when considering how he reacted to being placed in an enclosure at the groomers. Unfortunately, there was no way of knowing for sure. Truthfully, it didn't matter that much to me, although I was curious about what had befallen William and wanted to have a better understanding of him. What was important was what we did moving forward to solve the problems.

His poor aching hips were so bad it was painful watching him slowly slump down on all fours. It took a great effort on his part. He'd get about two-thirds of the way down and give up and let himself flop the rest of the way. He never bothered trying to sit. It was too painful for him.

Christine's priority was getting William's teeth taken care of. I was concerned, however, about having William go through anesthesia at his age. I wasn't sure he'd survive.

Christine countered, "If we don't take care of his teeth, they're only going to get worse. If they get worse, he may stop eating. That will lead to a long-drawn-out death for him."

She could tell I was struggling. "Tom, old age is not a disease."

"What do you mean?"

"You're worried about his age, but old age isn't the problem. Let's start by taking care of his problems. That will make him more comfortable, and the first one is his mouth."

From the first time I met her I was a fan of Christine's shoot-from-the-hip manner. She wasn't always gentle; sometimes she was just plain abrupt, but I appreciated her candor. It was refreshing. It was also reason enough for me to rely on her when it came to difficult decisions. So I scheduled William for dental surgery with her a couple of days later.

When the day came, I crossed my fingers and put my faith in Christine. I believed she was right. His mouth would only get worse if we did nothing. I tried to convince myself that if

William didn't make it through, it was probably for the best. At least he wouldn't be in pain any longer.

But William came through even better than I'd hoped, and once again Christine proved the importance of having a good veterinarian on your side. She was essential to any success we'd have with William. I took comfort in knowing she'd always be there for William, for Atticus, who was aging as well, and for me.

William's dental work made a marked difference. Before, he'd wince when eating some food, but since the work was done, he was in less pain. On a clear Saturday morning after we all had breakfast, Atticus was leading us on a slow walk in a green field along the Saco River.

William couldn't go very far, nor could he go fast, but he was following Atticus and seemed happy with the warm sunshine on his body. About ten minutes along William stopped and without warning flopped over on his side. He tried to keep his head up, but he couldn't even do that. He lay flat in the high grass beside the trail and stopped moving.

I carried him as rapidly as I could across the field while Atticus trotted beside us. William appeared paralyzed.

Not a day went by when I hadn't thought about euthanasia, but here I was running toward our car and telling him, "Don't you die. Not so soon. Not yet!"

"It's one of two things," Christine O'Connell told me in the examination room. "It's either a stroke or something called old dog's vestibular disease. We should know within three days. If it's ODVD, it will dissipate, and he'll mostly be okay again. There may be a lingering head tilt and some other signs. If it's a stroke, we'll . . . Well, let's just hope it's not a stroke."

When I laid William on his bed at home, I covered him with a towel warmed in the dryer. The fire, rage, and distrust had left his eyes, replaced by a vacant watery sadness. I lifted his head and placed it on the back of my hand. Our eyes met. What I saw was helplessness.

Throughout the next day and a half, I did everything for William. I tried feeding him by hand, but he didn't eat much. I propped his head up so he could drink from a shallow dish. I carried him outside every three hours while holding him up when he went to the bathroom. When I did this, his head flopped to one side. There were no fights when I brought him up and down the stairs. Instead, I hugged his head against chest with my free hand.

That first night Atticus and I slept on the floor next to William's bed. I wanted him to know he wasn't alone.

The next day passed as the previous one had. There was no improvement. When William slept I took Atticus for a walk, or I'd do chores around the house, but whenever he woke up, I lay next to him and Atticus would lie down next to me. I continued to place William's head on my hand, and he would keep it there.

When it was time for bed on the second night after his incident, I decided not to sleep on the floor again because I hadn't slept well the night before. I placed William in his bed and took one of my unwashed hiking shirts, folded it, and placed it under his head for a pillow. I wanted him to have my scent with him. I kissed his forehead and covered him up.

Atticus and I slept up in our bed, five feet away. Looking out the window, I watched the stars above us. I prayed for guidance, patience, and acceptance. I prayed for the wisdom to be able to do the right thing at the right time. Mostly, though, I prayed for William. Not for him to live or to die, but to be without pain throughout his body. And I prayed for his suffering heart. He didn't ask to be left behind or to live with someone he didn't know. He didn't ask to be neglected or forgotten or discarded or left off in some strange place when he got old. He didn't ask for the pain in his body, the way his teeth were rotting, the way his hips ached so much he couldn't sit down. He didn't ask for any of it.

When I woke up with the rising sun, I looked over at William's bed. He was gone.

But where? And how?

I swung my legs over the edge of the bed, and that's when I saw him. I sat still, not knowing what to think. Atticus hopped to the bench at the foot of the bed and then onto the floor and went over to William. It was the first time he'd approached him. He looked down at him, and then up at me.

The little white body was as still as could be. Time stopped. I held my breath as if it would help. Eventually, the slow rise of his chest came. He was breathing.

But how did he do it?

Somehow during the night, William dragged a body that couldn't move to the side of the bed and slept beside and below where my head was. He was as close as he could get to me. His nose was nuzzled into my hiking shirt, which he had hauled along with him.

It would take several more days for William to walk on his own again. For the rest of his life, his head would often slant to one side, but the most important healing had nothing to do with his body.

It was clear to me that William had made a choice to live again. He was reaching out.

There are lyrics in the late Leonard Cohen's song "Anthem" that are perfect for what transpired that weekend. "There's a crack in everything. That's how the light gets in."

That's the way it was with William. The crack brought the light, and the light brought a new chance, and the chance brought a new beginning with new friends and a new voyage was born.

Something else had changed on that May morning.

There was no more William. There was only a Will, and his desire to live.

Once again, spring was following winter.

2

A Mack Truck Full
of Crazy

This is the great lesson of "Beauty and the
Beast," a thing must be loved before it is
lovable.
—G. K. CHESTERTON

Will had decided he wanted to live. But I had no idea
what to do with him, or how long he would live. Our
troubled start was nothing like I had expected. His rage was a
surprise. I knew it came out of pain and fear, but I wasn't sure
I was equipped for it.

I didn't know what to do for him, so I thought back to

when Atticus was a puppy. Paige Foster had suggested I carry him wherever we went the first month we were together. That obviously wasn't going to happen with Will, because he seemed to take me as a threat. So I tried to think of other ways to reach out to Will. One of them, an obvious choice, was to respect him and allow him to be himself.

All I ever wanted for Atticus was to simply be Atticus. I hoped he'd be his own dog as much as I was my own man. I wanted him to have choices. Meaning no disrespect to the likes of Cesar Millan, Patricia McConnell, the Monks of New Skete, and other published dog experts, I wasn't interested in raising a dog. I set out to raise an individual. That was the way I prepared Atticus for the world. With Will, I wished to do the same, but with obvious differences.

I was ignoring the contemporary professionals on animal behavior and relying instead on a pair of fellows from Concord, Massachusetts, named Ralph Waldo Emerson and Henry David Thoreau. I suppose that might make me the only person to ever nurture first a puppy and then an angry old dog on the tenets of transcendentalism.

In 1830 Emerson wrote in his journal, "In all my lectures I have taught one doctrine, namely, the infinitude of the private man."

How grand is that? *Infinitude*.

It speaks of endless possibilities for the individual so he or she can flourish and make more of a contribution to the world.

Emerson was a proponent of the individual, believing that government, the education system, organized religion, and society exerted pressures on people to always conform. He also noted, "Whoso would be a man must be a nonconformist."

This is how I raised Atticus, and what I wanted for Will.

If a person's individuality could be respected and celebrated, I reasoned, why not an animal's?

Atticus and I learned together, and I wanted the same thing for Will. I hoped we'd grow through authentic experiences.

I've always believed it was naive to think that every lion is exactly like every other lion, or every black bear is the same, or that each fox is a clone to all the others. I'm not deeply knowledgeable about science, but common sense and my own experience tell me this is true.

I have always believed in this, to some extent, which is why when Max died it was silly for me to go looking for another version of him. As it turns out, Atticus and Max couldn't have been any more different. I don't ascribe all those differences to the way they were nurtured. I think it also has to do with nature. And yet they were of the same breed.

Will was also of the same breed, but the three of them had nothing in common, other than—me.

Similarly, I am the youngest of nine siblings. Although we share blood and the same upbringing, I have little in common with my brothers and sisters, and many of them have little in common with one another. Like dogs of the same breed, we may look alike, but we don't act alike. There is nothing wrong with any of that—nothing wrong with them or me. It's just the way life plays out. *Vive la différence!*

I didn't set out to change the world by the way I raised Atticus. I wanted only to live in a way that would work for the two of us. It was a private choice for our private lives.

It's ironic that I am at the point where I don't give much thought to dog breeds. Any kind of "breedism" conflicts with my deeply held beliefs. And yet I've now lived with three miniature Schnauzers. But that has more to do with dear old fate than it does my wishes. Max needed a home, so I took him in, not really knowing what a miniature Schnauzer was. I had to look up the breed online after I agreed to take Max in sight unseen. When I figured it out, I cringed. I considered myself more a Black Lab man. Atticus came into my life because I went in search for another Max. And Will, well, you know by now why I took him in. It wasn't the breed. What mattered was that it was reported he was good with other dogs, and more important, he desperately needed a place to die with dignity.

One morning last year when I was shopping in North Conway's Four Your Paws Only, I was approached by a woman.

"Tom!"

"Yes." I didn't know her.

She pressed closer and leaned in, like we were coconspirators. "You and I have something in common."

"Oh?" I stepped back. "What's that?"

"We're both Schnauzer people!"

"Oh, um, I'm not really a *Schnauzer* person."

"Now that's funny!"

"No, seriously, I'm not. I know it may not seem that way, but the whole breed thing doesn't mean much to me."

She stopped for a moment and settled on a compromise. "Okay, but at least you're a dog person. Just like me!"

"Actually, I'm not really a dog person either."

She cocked her head to one side. Her forehead wrinkled.

"If you really need to say I'm something, you could say I'm an elephant person."

"An elephant person? But you live with two dogs."

"That's because I don't have room for two elephants."

But even if I did, I wouldn't treat them as elephants. First and foremost, they'd be individuals. I'd treat them as I have always treated Atticus and Max, and finally, Will.

After much education from the animals I've known, I would say that yes, dogs of the same breed share many physical traits and are susceptible to comparable health issues, and of course they can look similar, but that's where it ends. I no more think every Schnauzer is alike, or every beagle or poodle or bulldog for that matter, than I think every Kenyan, Croatian, American, Republican, Catholic, Jew, Democrat, vegan, hunter, Bostonian, Kansan, or New Yorker is exactly like all his or her counterparts.

O f course I shared none of this with Will, not that he could hear me pontificate or would want to listen. He was having a difficult enough time trying not to fall down. While he recovered, he slept most of his days away, and when he was awake he didn't want much of anything to do with Atticus or me. He wanted to be left alone.

Atticus and I would return from a walk and I'd see Will curled up in his bed in the corner. He'd raise an eyelid, see that we were home, and ignore us. When he did get up and move around our apartment, he didn't interact with us or look at us. When he became a little more mobile, he'd go into the bedroom to get away from us.

During a telephone conversation with my aunt Marijane, I said, "I want to help him, I just don't know how."

"Tommy, sometimes the only thing you can do in hospice is be there for someone. They've come to a great reckoning in their lives and they have to figure things out. You can't take it personally."

"Hospice?"

"That's what you are doing for Will, isn't it? Offering him hospice? Didn't you say you wanted to give him a place to die with dignity?"

That's exactly what I was doing, but the term hadn't crossed my mind.

"Tommy, you are giving him a sacrament," she added.

Marijane was a desert flower of mysticism, insight, compassion, and empathy. She was such a visionary that in 1977 *People* magazine wrote about her work.

When she was young she became a nun in the Franciscan Missionaries of Mary and earned a nursing degree, specializing in helping the disabled. She had never been farther than an hour outside of Boston when, as a thirty-three-year-old, she was sent to St. Michael's, Arizona, in the middle of the Navajo Nation to take care of another nun who was dying of cancer. There was only so much she could do for her patient, so she began to walk among the Navajo people and talk with them the best she could with her strong Boston accent.

It wasn't long before she had a second patient. A Navajo family brought their polio-stricken eight-year-old son to her. She worked with him for months with little success, observed constantly by a Navajo medicine man from atop his horse. Every day he'd watch silently as she put the boy through exercises. His silence drove Marijane crazy, because she was outgoing by nature. Back in Boston, many of the other nuns called her "Maria" after the Julie Andrews character in *The Sound of Music*. Ebullient and youthfully innocent, she played the guitar, liked being active, and laughed with ease—and she was pretty.

One day, finally, her polio patient was able to stand up on his own by using two chairs. The silent medicine man watched intently, then road away as fast as his horse could carry him, but returned quickly, bringing his three-year-old grandchild, who suffered with cerebral palsy.

Within a few months, Marijane was working with twenty-five patients. She immersed herself in the Navajo culture and founded St. Michael's Special Education School, which created change throughout the Navajo Nation. In return, she was changed by their culture.

The Navajo people fell in love with Marijane—but they weren't alone. She was witty, bright, and kind, but her most endearing quality was her rare ability of looking into another, seeing his or her darkest side, and responding without judgment.

Many were surprised when she left the Church and St. Michael's, although she always stayed close to the people she met, returning often to visit with them. She went on to receive a degree in psychology and worked in hospice.

After my father died, Marijane and I became close. She was in Arizona, a Phoenix Suns fan, and I was in New Hampshire, a Boston Celtics fan. We'd joke and joust when the teams played each other.

When *Following Atticus* was published, I flew Marijane out to join Atticus and me for several days along our book tour. It's something I would have wanted to do with my father. Although he wouldn't have accepted the offer, secretly he would have been pleased that I wanted him along with Atticus and me. So instead I asked Marijane to join us.

She and I had never spent much time in each other's company except at an occasional family reunion. But we'd spoken and e-mailed often, and after we spent three straight days together, our connection was fortified.

My family had splintered when my mother died. We were never close, and I longed for any kind of intimacy with them, but, as Marijane would say, some people don't have a lot to give. They do the best they can. "Sometimes I'm surprised some of your brothers and sisters are able to sit up and take nourishment. You kids didn't have it easy."

She'd also say, "I don't envy your father either. I wouldn't want to walk a mile in his moccasins."

Many times she told me the story of how after my mother died, he'd call her out on the reservation late at night and all he could do was cry. It would last for as long as thirty minutes. "I'd answer the phone. Jack couldn't talk. All he had to give were tears. We did a lot of that the first year. He'd call and cry. I would listen, and inside I'd cry for my brother."

At the conclusion of every one of our conversations, or in closing each e-mail, Marijane would end with "Walk in beauty." At first I thought it was from the Byron poem, but she later explained that it had to do with living in a loving way toward the world. The Navajo told her that she "walked in beauty" because of the way she danced with the natural world and all its peoples and animals and gave freely of her heart.

During her trip east for our book tour, Marijane was fascinated by Atticus. He would sit on her lap in the front passenger seat, as if they'd always known each other. At the end of each day, when we'd say good night, she'd say, "Good night, Tommy, walk in beauty. Good night, Atticus, walk in beauty." She talked to him like I did, as a peer, and I appreciated that.

When she arrived home in Phoenix and Atticus and I continued on our tour, we would talk after each event. She wanted to know how things went, how many people showed up, and how they responded to my talk. Late one night, after we said good night, she sent me an e-mail that greeted me in the morning.

"You know I love dogs. I've lived with some wonderful companions, and I can never pass a dog without saying hello. But Atticus is very unusual. He's the one who walks in beauty. He's what I'm trying to be more like. I know you don't talk about him in that way, but you know it's true. Spending those days with you two was very special to me. I think Jack was smiling down on us. I love you both, please pass that on to Atticus."

When Will came to live with us, Marijane asked questions about his mood, his health—she wanted the smallest bits of information. When I let her know that Atticus was keeping his distance, being respectful but not warm, she said, "He's waiting until he's needed. You'll see."

With Marijane as a role model, I became less judgmental of others and myself, but understood I had a long way to go. I asked Marijane what she would do if she were with us, and she said, "You're already doing it. I see you putting yourself in his moccasins all the time. Have faith. He's been through a lot."

When I told Marijane about an old girlfriend, she listened and waited until I was done, then responded, "You know, Tommy, none of us are perfect, but be careful of the ones driving a Mack truck full of crazy."

That was one of the differences between Marijane and me. While we both could see a Mack truck full of crazy coming our way, she didn't judge the person. She protected herself, but also offered compassion and understanding, if only in the form of prayers. I would never hear her belittle anyone. She would talk about getting angry with someone, but I never witnessed her being judgmental.

Most of Will's past was a mystery, but whenever Marijane and I discussed his challenges after that, we'd remind each other that he'd been run over by a Mack truck full of crazy. My job was to let him know that it would never hurt him again.

"You have it right," Marijane wrote to me. "Dogs and coyotes and owls and bears and people are all the same inside. We have the same emotions. We fear and love and get angry and are happy. We all have compassion and empathy. People like to say that dogs live in the moment. I think some do— like some people do—but look at Will, he's not living in the moment. He's tormented by his past. I admire that you treat Atticus like you do. It's worked. I have to believe it will eventually work with Will, too. Just remember that you can only do your best."

Whenever Will attacked me in the coming months, I'd lead with my heart instead of my ego. I tried not to take it personally, but it was hard to take a Zen approach whenever he tried to bite me in the face. I decided it was best not to expect anything; instead I concentrated on giving, and nothing else.

Will's appetite grew, which thrilled me because as May ended and the first week of June bloomed, he still shivered as he stood outside each morning. If by chance he lasted throughout the summer, Will was going to need some natural insulation.

To help him put on weight, I added oil to his meals, gave

him vitamins and supplements for his hips, and put his food and water in elevated bowls, which put less stress on his neck and legs and made swallowing easier. I gave Will three meals a day, which wasn't lost on Atticus, who ate two, and when I started to see Will's belly start to plump, I took it as a victory.

Is it strange to say I enjoyed watching him eat? He would look at me as I put the food down and then tuck in, as if it was all that mattered to him. Perhaps he was learning to live in the moment after all. When he'd finish eating, he'd take endless draughts of water. It would go on and on . . . and on. It was almost comical how much he drank. But Will always seemed sort of dried out to me, and I wanted him to hydrate.

Under his white hair, his skin was dry, and as often as he drank, he reminded me of someone who had been stuck in the desert without any water. He was a sponge, and I refilled the bowl three times as often as I used to when it was just Atticus and me.

Of course, the more water he drank, the more he urinated, and no matter how often I got him outside, there would rarely be a day when he didn't go in the house. But he needed water, and water he got.

A few friends suggested diapers for dogs, but his skin was sensitive and prone to breaking down. I noticed how during that first summer his skin started to flake and then scabbed and became crusty. So I started him on medicated shampoo. I worried that diapers would cause more skin problems. Another friend suggested the same puppy pads I'd put down for Atticus ten years earlier, but it's not as if Will gave much thought to where he'd piss. He'd go as if he suddenly remembered, "Oh yeah, I have to go. This seems like a fine spot."

There were many snacks, but these sometimes highlighted what a strange past Will had before his life in Jackson. When I gave Atticus an eight-inch-long chew stick, he leaped up onto his side of the couch, grabbed it between his front paws, and began to gnaw on it methodically. Will didn't have a clue what to do with his. I reached out and he took it in his mouth, but then he proceeded to walk around the living room with it clenched between his teeth, jutting out of the side of his mouth as if he were W. C. Fields chewing on a cigar.

I sat on the floor, he walked up to me, I mussed his hair, and I said, "Here, Will, let me help you with that."

When I reached out to hold it on one end so he could chew the other, he struck with those quick teeth and bit the back of my hand. Once again, he drew blood.

He may not have known what to do with that chew stick, and he'd never learn no matter how many times I offered him one, but he always seemed to know exactly what to do with my hand.

While Will was struggling to find his new place in life, it was frustrating for Atticus and painful and exhausting for me. But I started to laugh about such things. Even when he bit me that day I caught myself saying, "You son of a . . . !" and then a great boom of laughter rose from my belly. Will led me to learn that the basest swears can be charming when accompanied by loud laughter.

I was beginning to understand that Will was just being Will. Isn't that what I wanted for him?

He was learning about a new life in a new home, and I was learning patience and compassion just when they were most difficult to grasp. With Will in mind, I taped my favorite Thomas Merton quote on the refrigerator: "The beginning of love is the will to let those we love be perfectly themselves, the resolution not to twist them to fit our own image."

I'd pause to read it whenever I opened the refrigerator door. It became scripture for me, and an affirmation to allow Will to be Will, no matter what form that took.

While negotiating the challenges of a life with Will, and nursing him through the days when I feared losing him, I had to admit I was already falling in love with the old fellow, even if he could be a son of a bitch at times.

I bought three cheap area rugs and placed one on the wood floor in the living room. The others I put away for when the first one needed to go to the dump. I would much rather have gone without the rug, because wood was easier to clean, but Will needed the traction to help him stand.

I also purchased an electric steam mop for the wooden floors and the linoleum in the bathroom. For the area rug and the bedroom rug I bought a Bissell SpotBot. I placed it over wherever he urinated or defecated on the carpet, turned it on, and left it there. The machine rinsed the carpet, sprayed it with shampoo, scrubbed with a circular brush, rinsed it again, and then suctioned it all up. I'd leave it alone and come back ten minutes later when it had run through the cycle and shut off.

In an attempt to give Will his own space, I bought him a larger crate than the one I had for him when he first arrived. I packed it with soft bedding. But he so hated it that he screeched whenever I tried to put him in it. Even though I didn't shut the door, he'd start to shake and cry out. So both the small crate and the large one were sent off to the Conway Area Humane Society thrift store.

No matter what I did, there were many missing pieces to the puzzle of Will. Yet he improved here and there, and these little triumphs gave me glimpses of hope.

The harness I put on him during his first days allowed me to move him more easily and pick him up more safely; if I held him by the harness, he couldn't reach me with his teeth. And as time went on, Will wanted to be close to me when we were out in public. At the vet's, in a store, at the post office, Will seemed to look to me for comfort and protection. In a strange environment, I was part of his pack.

Whenever anyone has asked me what Atticus thought about when he sat high atop a mountain and gazed out at the horizon, as still as stone apart from his head and eyes, I'd say, "You'll have to ask him."

I never knew what he was thinking up there. Frankly, it's none of my business. I knew that I was always soaking in the majesty of the views, and maybe he was as well. But I'd always made it a point not to put words in his mouth or thoughts into his head. To pretend I knew them at such times would be a disservice to my friend. Allowing him the power of his choices didn't cost me anything.

I could tell you when he was hungry or thirsty or wanted me to lie down with him, or go outside, or go for a walk. He let me know when he didn't want to hike, because of weather or something else I couldn't figure out, and I'd always listened to him when this happened, and we turned back.

Early one summer day I drove to one of our favorite places to walk in the woods, under Whitehorse Ledge in North

Conway. Rather than heading up the trail as usual, Atticus hopped out of the car and sat down. He was letting me know he wasn't budging. I opened the car door and he jumped right back inside. I drove around the corner to Echo Lake. He did the same thing. I took us across town to Pudding Pond. He didn't even bother getting out of the car. Finally, when we arrived at Thorne Pond ten miles away, he was happy to walk.

His ability to say no has always pleased me, especially when we hiked together in the winter. I often heard from critics who were against him being on the mountains from December through March. They'd say something like "Dogs don't know any better. He just wants to make you happy, so he'll go wherever you lead him, even if it is dangerous."

"You don't know Atticus," I was always happy to say.

And lest anyone think I'm making him out to be some perfect higher being, I'm well aware of Atti's shortcomings. Toss him a treat and it would hit him in the forehead. Toss him a ball and he would duck. He'd plow through a foot of snow, but ask him to cross freshly mowed summer grass that's coated with morning dew and he would act as if he were walking through shards of glass. And while he climbed more mountains than most could ever imagine, and did it with such ease you'd think he was part mountain goat, he would become paralyzed when asked to walk up a set of stairs with open spaces between each step.

Atticus wasn't perfect, but like all of us, he was perfect at being himself.

As much as I knew about him, I couldn't tell you what he was thinking most of the time. Ask me how he felt, though, and I had a better chance of figuring that out. I knew when he was happy or not, or frightened or nervous or frustrated. But the same is true for people, isn't it? I usually can't tell you what my friends are thinking, but I can tell you how they're feeling. We wear our emotions, while our thoughts are our own.

Will was even more of a challenge than Atticus in this way, because we were just getting to know each other and I wouldn't dare try to guess his thoughts the majority of the time. Yet I could definitely tell you when he was angry. Happiness was trickier, though. Maybe it was the pain or the lack of trust or maybe he was depressed, but very seldom did I look at him and think about how content he was.

I'd regularly think of Paige Foster and how she'd say about Atti and me, "Y'all will work it out." I wondered if it would ever ring true for Will and me. Would he and I ever work it out?

There was much I didn't know and moments when I'd get so frustrated that I'd step outside just to breathe. Calming down, I always reverted to the simple question I asked when I was raising Atticus: *If I was in his place, what would I want?* This simple question left me open to whatever possibilities Will wanted to show me.

I appreciated Will's need for lengthy naps because it gave Atticus and me a chance to sneak out together, for a walk or a short hike or a drive to the store. I didn't want to sacrifice what Atticus and I had built because Will required so much of my attention. His naps gave us just enough freedom. We were no longer taking long hikes, because Will couldn't be left alone that long, but I was fine with that. I believe Atticus was too, since his body wasn't as nimble as it once was, and it took him longer to recover from a tough trek. Oftentimes I'd witness him with the slightest limp the day after hikes, and I noticed how he slept more deeply and later into the morning than in years past.

Whenever we left Will at home, I'd leave music playing. On a Saturday morning that first summer, a portable speaker sat on top of the coffee table. Will was sleeping on the area rug.

When Atticus and I returned an hour later, the soundtrack to the movie *August Rush* was playing, and Will wasn't where I'd left him. He was curled in a tiny ball and his left ear was pressed flat against the leg of the coffee table.

I had a thought. I reached over and turned off the music.

Will pulled his ear away from the leg of the table.

I turned it back on. He shifted his head and pressed it back against the leg. I turned it off, turned it on, again and again. Each time I turned it on Will pressed his ear to the table leg.

On February 1, 1924, the New York Symphony Orchestra played Beethoven's Ninth Symphony (including, of course, the "Ode to Joy") at Carnegie Hall. It was a live broadcast. According to *The Baten*, volumes 2–3, via Marcus Williams, in her home that night, Helen Keller was mesmerized by the sensations she discovered by putting her hands on the speaker of the radio; she could "feel, not only the vibrations, but also the impassioned rhythm, the throb and the urge of the music! The intertwined and intermingling vibrations enchanted me."

She added, "I also sensed, or thought I did, the tender sounds of nature that sing into my hand—swaying reeds and winds and the murmur of streams."

Helen Keller had a wondrous and courageous spirit, and I am awestruck at times in considering how she lived her life. Who was I to think Will would feel anything different or be anything less? So I moved forward with Will and my music experiments in the hope that he too would find "the tender sounds of nature" that would sing into his hand . . . along with the "swaying reeds and winds and the murmur of streams." I know he felt nature when we were in the backyard; I'd seen him give his undivided attention to a breeze or the warm sun on his back. I even noted that the bright yellow umbrella tops of dandelions caught the attention of his weak eyes.

Considering his physical condition, I would not be able to get Will to the top of a mountain. Yet I yearned to find ways to allow him to experience the full impact of nature. If the vibrations of music could help him feel the natural world, I would take it.

I decided to be more selective about what I left playing for Will when Atticus and I went out in the future. In the past I'd let my computer shuffle the songs in my collection, but classical music made sense to me for Will, with its flow and inspiration, and so did instrumental movie soundtracks. I would soon be enlisting Danny Elfman, John Williams, James Newton Howard, and Randy Newman to look after Will when we left him behind. I hoped their music to reach where I hadn't been able to. He might not have been able to *hear* it, but he could feel it. That's what I wanted for Will. I wanted him to feel life again.

Whenever I'd put him in his bed and cover him up, I'd have speakers nearby on the floor and choose melodies for him to drift off to, songs with words that lifted the soul. Lullabies, if you will. But I called them Willabies. There were love songs, by performers like James Taylor, Sarah Brightman, Frank Sinatra, Billie Holiday, and Barbra Streisand. I started to record videos of Will "listening" to music and shared them on our Facebook page. The videos showed an old, unwanted soul, draped with warm towels or blankets and with a pillow tucked gently under his head, settling down to sleep to the vibrations of music. Nearly every video would end the same way, with Will snoring peacefully. Who would have thought so many people would be moved to tears by a sleeping dog they would never meet?

What some folks might have found to be the inanest three minutes of boredom on the Internet turned out to be soothing to thousands of our fans, who took the simplest joy in watching the once unwanted and very broken Will give up his anger and surrender to a nurturing moment. The hundreds of comments left often spoke of how people longed for simple times and pleasures, when climbing into bed and pulling up the covers was the most wholesome thing in the world. They talked of being children again, of having bedtime stories read to them, of having someone look after them in the same manner. The most common refrain was "I pray that when I'm old like Will is, someone will do that for me." Watching Will slide away into a carefree dreamworld was sweet therapy for those with busy lives.

Music added to Will's life. It smoothed out some of his anger and let him feel loved. Like Helen Keller before him, he had a new way to receive the gifts of the world. And I'd received my first breakthrough as I learned a way to bring Will contentment.

As charming as people found the Willabies, and as happy as I was to have this new way to help Will experience life, no part of the process was simple. Because Will often shivered in bed as he slept, I'd started to cover him up, but he would startle and raise his hackles. I found that the trick was to first gently stroke my hand across his back, as softly as a feather. He'd open his eyes but would know what was coming. The next step was to take a heated towel or a small blanket or one of my fleece shirts and lay it over him, moving from his shoulders down to his hips. I learned that he'd jerk away if I started with his hips. Through trial and error I learned to do it in a manner that left him comfortably under his covers for hours.

I can't tell you what he was thinking, but ask me how he felt and I could give you many answers.

Anthropomorphism—the attribution of human motivations to animals—has a bad rap these days, and if it's taken too far I reject it as well. But it's an important step in our empathy with other species. Imagining what another being is going through helps us bridge a gap. And it was never too much of a reach to consider how I'd feel if I were shivering like Will.

For his daytime naps, I placed a dog biscuit on top of his blankets, not too far away from his nose. I wanted to believe that no matter what Will experienced in his past, there would now be a little magic waiting for him when he awakened.

3

The Bear Who
Followed Us Home

In a utilitarian age, of all other times, it is a
matter of grave importance that fairy tales
should be respected.
—CHARLES DICKENS

A bear followed us home one day. I could say it was an ordinary day, like any other, but I would be lying, and that
was even before the bear came along.

If you lived here, you'd know what I am talking about. It
was one of those fleeting White Mountain days found in mid
to late spring where you could sit for twelve hours in nature

and count a thousand shades of green, only to realize you'd missed at least a thousand more.

The early sunlight slanted through the forests and across the mountaintops to electrify all those shades of green. None of it registers in your eyes because it is impossible to grasp. It seems made up, illogical, and incomprehensible. No, it is far better to leave it up to the heart to fathom these dazzling displays of hope and growth when the brown and gray of winter are finally and completely overtaken by spring, before summer comes along and the mountains turn a consensus green.

It's easiest to watch this phenomenon from a distance—say, from the side or top of a mountain—but you can still see it as you walk throughout the valleys. No matter what troubles you, everything appears buoyant early on those kind of mornings when the night chill remains, and white cartoon clouds puff along like parade balloons in the deepest sea of blue you could ever picture yourself swimming in.

Atticus and I had left Will sleeping at home. We rose early to make sure he didn't have another accident, and then brought him back inside where he would sleep for a while, for sleeping is mostly what he did. He was good at it. And he was good at tuning us out and pretending we weren't there.

We had just crossed the covered bridge on our way home when we heard the excited clamor of tourists. One word rose above all the chatter.

"Bear!"

A man behind us, standing in the middle of the bridge with his camera, yelled to say the bear was coming our way, but we kept walking, because we understood the ways of bears in Jackson.

We heard him crashing through the shrubs lining the

Wildcat River before we saw him. A flash of shiny black fur burst through the brush ten feet in front of us. He was young, all legs and nervous energy, and ready to dash across the road. Strangely, though, he stopped. His body tightened like a spring, and he turned to watch us as we kept walking toward him. Instantly, the spring released and he was off, dashing across the road in an awkward galumphing trot as cars stopped to let him pass. Tourists had their cameras and phones out and raced to get a photograph, but he was too fast for any of them. Still, seeing a bear gave them something to tell their friends back home.

Atticus and I were used to seeing bears, and I thought of this as yet another reason I love living halfway to wild. That morning, though, I had a lot on my mind, and it all came down to Will.

Our home was no longer peaceful. Atticus walked gingerly from the bedroom each morning, poised to avoid a Will accident. Then there was Will's temper. He was getting better in that he was eating healthier and sleeping more, and he didn't attack quite as much when I tried to help him. But he could still erupt at any moment, and I had the fresh scars to prove it.

I needed to find a balance at home—a way where Will was happier and Atticus and I could feel as if we had a home again.

Two hundred yards down the road, a foursome of golfers yelled out as the young bear raced across their putting green.

Those golfers would have stories to tell sitting around the nineteenth hole in the hours to come. Can't you imagine the conversations, and the excuses?

"I would have had that birdie had that darn bear not kicked the ball while it was on its way to the hole."

A tenth of a mile from our house I heard the thumping

of feet, and for the third time the bear crossed in front of us, looking more silly than menacing. He went into the brush behind another house, and I guessed he was heading down to the river, to wherever his den was.

Back at home, I woke up Will by gently rocking him. When he looked at me, I brought him up to his feet, holding him by his harness so he wouldn't fall over. During his recovery, he accepted me holding him slightly longer and didn't take exception to my assistance. Outside, I placed him on the grass on the small rise in the middle of our backyard. He stumbled for a few steps, and I steadied him. Then, cautiously but a bit drunkenly, he started circling.

Since his episode of what had turned out to be old dog vestibular disease a month earlier, his held tilt was pronounced and he had a difficult time walking a straight line unless he was following Atticus or me or walking to me, or was in the house and had landmarks to help him navigate. That head tilt had him walking in crooked circles, like a boat whose rudder is turned all the way to the right.

Atticus no longer felt comfortable on the grass, not since Will arrived. You see, Atticus had never gone to the bathroom on the lawn. He'd mark a tree along the property line, and he never defecated on our property. He always waited until we were on a walk. But Will went everywhere. If Atticus had a reason to cross the yard, it was as if he was tiptoeing through a minefield. Mostly he skirted the property line.

Will circled under the warming sun and took a myopic view of whatever he looked at, like an elderly professor studying a small wildflower. I grabbed a rake to clean up some leaves left over from the fall. I saw Atticus walk from under the trees toward Will, and this surprised me. He stopped halfway to him, turned his back, and faced the vacant yard to the north.

There was that same young bear we'd seen on our walk. He was a yearling, standing like a huge puppy.

"Atticus, you don't know him. Remember to be gentle."

With that, Atticus sat, and so did the bear, only twenty feet away.

I trusted Atticus, who hadn't worn a leash and collar for years, but still, I wanted him to be cautious. "Be careful, my friend."

Atticus dropped to a sphinx position. Will was oblivious to anything going on as he continued making his circles, but I was aware that Atticus had placed himself between Will and the bear. And I understood that although he was displeased with Will and may not have respected his manners, this is where Atticus would play a role in Will's life. From a distance he watched over Will, definitely not approving of his attacks on me and disgusted by his personal habits, but seeming to understand his own role as protector.

I'd seen him do this once before. It was on the day Will collapsed, when we were waiting to see Christine O'Connell. Atticus sat on a couch in the waiting room. I was next to him, holding Will in my arms. A man and a large dog came in the front door. Atticus gave a growl and his hackles stood on end.

"Whoa, Atti! What's that about?"

He had never growled at another animal before. The other dog backed up, and Atticus relaxed. When the dog took a few steps forward, Atticus growled again. He was protecting Will, even though he didn't like him.

In the backyard, the bear mimicked Atticus by slipping down into the same position. The two looked at each other, and there was no tension or signs of menace or aggression. I took a photo.

The older bears who live near us had always made their way up from the Ellis River along the bear path, and then across the lawn on the way to the local inns and restaurants. I didn't mind them because they mostly avoided us. But I could tell by his size and his awkwardness that this fellow had only recently been forced out into the world by his mother. Year-lings are unpredictable. They are new to the world on their own and need to find their way in life. I didn't want this young fellow to get too comfortable around us, so I chased him off by yelling and moving toward him.

He disappeared into the woods, and we went inside.

W ill may no longer have fought me whenever I picked him up and carried him up and down the stairs, and seemed to understand it was what he needed, but once we were in our apartment, things were different.

Will would be as calm as could be in my arms, but I'd warn Atticus that I was going to put him down. Atticus would hop up on the couch, where he was safe. I'd place Will on the throw rug, and the demon dance would start. Anger bubbled to the surface. He'd rear up on his hind legs and spin around, trying to leap at me, snarling, baring his teeth, looking to bite. I'd move quickly out of his reach. Will would become so fierce he'd lose control, toppling over on his side, and his weakness would anger him all the more.

As strange as it may seem, I felt Will had a right to be an-gry. I even respected it, although I despised being his constant target and hated the bites.

It didn't matter that Will couldn't hear me. I often told him he could stay angry for as long as he needed to and that someday . . . Well, there might come a day when he didn't feel the need to be angry, and that would be okay too.

The arc of his temper was predictable. He would calm down within a minute of the frenzy as his yelps turned to growls, which turned to grumbles. After the grumbles came the snores as his tantrums wore him out, and he'd fall asleep where he fell.

The morning the bear followed us home, Will threw his regular tantrum after I brought him upstairs. Soon he was asleep again, and when I looked out the window, the yearling was looking up at me. I grabbed two pans and ran outside yelling and clashing them together like cymbals. He bolted.

There are basic rules I follow with our neighboring bears: I don't leave trash where they can get into it, I don't feed them, and whenever we are in close proximity to each other, I make certain we each have escape routes. But I set firmer boundaries with the younger bears. Whenever they are near, I chase them away. Knowing to keep their distance from humans could save their lives.

There is saying that "a fed bear is a dead bear." If you feed bears, they will keep coming back for more until it becomes dangerous, and then something has to be done to the bear. The first step is relocating the bear, but if problems persist, they will eventually be destroyed, which is a shame since in most cases it could all be avoided if people didn't feed them. I respect my role in the relationship with the local bears and always remember that they are not my friends, they're wild animals. But I also defended their right to pass through the yard. This was their land before settlers took it away from them by developing towns, and who was I to tell them where they could and couldn't go?

So I knew how to handle bears, but Will was a real challenge. Not a day passed when I didn't feel overwhelmed by his physical, mental, and emotional needs. I regularly tried to put myself in his place; that's why I respected his anger. But switching from the peaceful life with Atticus to the messy one Will had brought to our home was difficult, and I often wondered if I was up to the challenge.

On that morning of the yearling, while watching Will after he fell on his side, his eyes wild and his teeth showing, a memory surfaced of a place I used to know. When I was getting ready to start the *Undertoad,* I needed a job. A nursing home in a town close to Newburyport was hiring.

It was a dreadful place. It reeked of loneliness and desperation, of pain and suffering. If I were elderly, I'd rather be dead than end up there. Even nicer nursing homes can still be depressing, but this was the lowest level. It's where people ended up because they had no money and no one to care about them. Only a handful of the residents who had family in the area who visited them often could be considered fortunate. The rest were the forsaken and the forgotten.

Sadness showed in the dim lighting, in the old tile floors covered with years of film, in the dreary paint on the walls and the cheap wood paneling. It was evident in every aspect of the building and it was reflected in the faces of the residents. It even showed in many of the staff members.

The shifts were often understaffed, and it is charitable to say that those who worked there had had rough lives themselves. I was the only man working there, and many of the women showed up for work each morning hungover. Some had fresh bruises. Sometimes, when I arrived at work, I'd see that some of the silent residents, the ones who wouldn't or couldn't talk, also had bruises. It was not a kind place, although you could find occasional kindnesses if you looked for them. Mostly, though, the staff was not much better off than the residents they were poorly paid to care for. It was a fellowship of dejection. The only differences were that the residents were older than the employees and the employees were free to leave after their shifts were over.

A director had recently been hired to turn the facility around, to make it respectable again. She was the one who hired me.

She had a virtuous heart and a kind smile, but her husband was dying of cancer and she had little energy to give to the place. When she noticed that the man she brought on to help with exercises was getting the residents to open up in different ways, she gave me more freedom to let me do whatever I wanted.

My coworkers weren't sure what to think of me. I was the only person doing rehab work, which they considered a glamorous position. It was a natural fit since I'd taken some courses on rehabilitation in college. They didn't take kindly to the fact that a newcomer had landed that job, and they couldn't relate to me because I didn't go out drinking with them at night, and instead of sitting outside smoking cigarettes at lunch, I'd sit in the lounge or under a tree and read. No matter our differences, I liked many of them.

A few weeks after I was hired, I was called to Eunice Sharpwood's room. She was in her early nineties but robust and bright. She was also ornery. The assistant director purposely chose a roommate for her who was deaf and couldn't speak and seemed completely unaware of anything that happened around her. Whenever Eunice launched into one of her tirades, her roommate would do what she always did—look out the window without a twitch or even a blink, no matter what outrageous things Eunice said or did.

On that day, with Eunice screaming at people to get away from her, her jowls shaking, her eyes ablaze, her cane wielded like a sword, I surprised her by asking, "Eunice, why are you always so angry?"

The rest of the staff looked at me like I was an idiot. *Why would you even care? Just subdue her, moron!*

She lowered her cane, surprised that someone had asked her something. "Why? I'll tell you why! Because no one will dance with me!"

"I didn't know you liked to dance."

"That's the problem! No one here knows anything about me because none of you care. No one cares!"

That day at lunch, when the residents gathered in the dining room, I turned on some Sinatra and approached Eunice. "Mrs. Sharpwood, may I have this dance?"

Stone silence. Eventually, she let her defenses down and said, "It's about time." But then she smiled and took my hand. We hung her cane on my forearm, and we danced. She was far better at it than I was, and compared to me, she was nimble. Eunice closed her eyes. Contentment washed over her face. I imagined her young again and thought about how much fun she must have had when she danced.

As the song came to a close, I started to wobble, as though exhausted by our dance. I handed Eunice her cane, and I collapsed onto the floor.

"You, my dear, have worn me out!" I then made a show of fainting.

Eunice smiled again, and jiggled as she laughed. She bent over me and stared. When I opened my eye to look up at her, she hit me with her cane, "Like hell I have. Get up. We're not done yet."

That day, the dining room of the woebegone nursing home saw more laughter in it than it had in a long time.

Eunice wasn't the only one there who felt as if no one cared. As I spent time with the residents and helped them with their exercises, I began to see each person differently. One was Mrs. Fish, who rarely spoke and did so in a whisper. When I finished some range-of-motion exercises with her one afternoon, I took my hand off her arm and gently touched her face. She barely moved but looked toward my hand.

"Abigail, can you tell me about your first kiss?"

She looked back down at her lap. She looked hollow. But ever so slowly the slightest smile appeared. She closed her eyes and leaned her head back. She placed her hand on top of mine. "I was ten. His name was Johnny Appleton. We were on a hayride." She opened her eyes, and like Eunice's before her, they were young again. She began to talk, and I listened.

I don't think I've stopped listening since.

My coworkers didn't take kindly to my laughter. The more I learned about the residents, and the more I listened when they told me their stories, the more we found to laugh about.

That day three years ago when the bear followed us home, I thought about Eunice Sharpwood for the first time in close to fifteen years, and I came to understand what I needed to do with Will. Like Eunice, and the rest of the residents of that depressing nursing home, I had to discover what brought him back to life, what made him smile. I had to help him learn to dance again.

The enchanted forest had helped me discover who I was, and I hoped it would also help Will. I knew Atticus would contribute in his unique way, keeping his distance until he was needed while providing a calming presence. So would the lessons I'd learned from Paige Foster, the breeder who brought Atticus into my life.

And of course there was the influence of Aunt Marijane—her experience with the disabled Navajo children, her understanding of Jung, her mysticism, and her years working hospice.

Now I was summoning the memories of the once-forgotten elderly who had taught me much in the few months I worked with them at the nursing home. Those dear people, surely long dead, would—in their way—help me help Will. For he was no different from them—a senior citizen, left behind, mostly forgotten. He deserved the respect we should pay all our elders. My goal was to treat him as I treated them—with dignity.

T he yearling did not stay away for long. He returned repeatedly, no matter how often I chased him away. As he grew, he would always make his presence known, but never in a troublesome way. I'd see him watching us from the woods, or walking near us when Atticus and I were out together. He'd weave in and out of the trees, but if anyone else was ever near us, he'd vanish, only to reappear over time when it was just Atticus and me, and sometimes Will.

When I next called Marijane, I said, "A bear followed us home the other day."

"A bear? Tommy! A bear? What happened? Was he a threat? Are Atticus and Will okay?"

"We were out on a walk and a yearling followed us home. He was drawn to Atticus, I think. When Atti sat, so did the bear. When Atti lay down, the bear did too."

There was silence on the other end of the phone. She was contemplating what I was saying. When Marijane met Atticus, she watched him closely as she approached him. When she reached out to pet him, she stopped. She pulled her hand back and grew serious, and studied him as she studied everyone. He mirrored her. A silent connection existed between them.

Later in the day, after she'd watched Atticus and me interacting for several hours, she repeated something my father had said about Atti: "Are you sure he's a dog?" But Marijane added the Navajo spin to it: "He's like a medicine man. He has a deep spirituality."

So when I described Atticus's interaction with the yearling, she understood the calmness between the two of them.

"I've decided to call him Aragorn," I said.

"Aragorn?"

"A Tolkien character from *The Lord of the Rings*. In the beginning, he's a common man who feels at home in nature. Over time you learn he's the heir to the throne."

"I think that yearling has a lot to live up to," and she laughed.

"I see something different in him, different like I can't put my finger on it. In a way, he reminds me of a young Atticus."

Will's fairy tale began with an unwanted and fateful twist; then came a journey to a faraway land next to an enchanted forest, where he'd meet others who would help him;

and now even a bear was involved. Not a talking bear, mind you, as you might expect in a fairy tale, but a bear nonetheless.

Our lives were chaotic in those first months, and I often felt lost. But I came to think that we had fallen into that indefinable place Kentucky poet Wendell Berry wrote of in *The Real Work*: "It may be that when we no longer know what to do, we have come to our real work, and when we no longer know which way to go, we have begun our journey."

4

Be Gentle

The more clearly we can focus our attention
on the wonders and realities of the universe
about us, the less taste we shall have for
destruction.

—RACHEL CARSON, from a speech accepting the
John Burroughs medal (April 1952)

I raised Atticus to be gentle and kind with other animals.
I've always been this way, believing animals deserve kindness whenever it's possible, which is nearly always, and at least
a measure of respect when it is not.

While one of my brothers spent his younger summers
sticking fireworks inside frogs at the local pond and tossing

them in the air to watch them explode, or pulling wings off of flies during boring sermons at church, I would sit in the same uncomfortable wooden pew playing with the flies who landed on my hands.

I remember crying as a six-year-old when my family went to Montreal for the World's Fair, Expo '67. The A-frame chalet we stayed in was visited by the friendliest rabbit, who let us pet him. I didn't want to leave him behind, not even for all the wonders we were about to witness. I cried and cried as my father made me get into the car.

All these years later, I am comfortable sharing one of the upper corners of our bathroom with a daddy longlegs each winter. In November one appears there. None of them have ever seemed to move, and I let them be. When the warmth of spring returns, they disappear.

There's a cliché spun again and again by many who love dogs. "They have so much to teach us." I agree with that, for I have learned much from the animals I've known. But I also believe we have much to teach them. For as long as people and dogs have been pairing up—about ten thousand years—it has been a symbiotic relationship. We teach each other. We take the lead in the civilized world while they often take the lead in the natural world. Together we have evolved into two species with a unique and universal friendship.

Some of it comes naturally; at other times there are lessons to learn and be reinforced.

One frozen November day during our second year of hiking, Atticus and I left Newburyport at six A.M. and drove the two and a half hours north to Crawford Notch. Soon after we arrived, I felt a little strange. Over the prior few weeks, my body had been feeling drunk and sluggish with a heaviness brought about by some unknown virus or bug. There were good days and some bad. It was an unpredictable cycle.

It came on during the first five minutes on the trail. My arms, legs, face, and lips felt numb—the same lethargy had visited me a few weeks earlier, at the beginning of a hike up Mount Chocorua. But after walking through the vibrant October woods and up the steep but short pitch to some open ledges, I left it behind. I felt fine the rest of the day.

I was hoping for a similar outcome on a ten-mile hike along the Willey Range covering three four-thousand-foot peaks—Field, Willey, and Tom. It's a trek we'd taken three times before, and one of my favorites. However, the farther along we walked, the worse I felt.

I tried to ignore it and concentrate on the crisp air, the snow on the side of the trail, the solitude of a weekday hike. Like Robert Frost in *My November Guest*, I took note of the trees and realized that somewhere through the years "I learned to know the love of bare November days . . ."

Even on flat sections of trail, I moved slowly. I thought about turning back but figured I could always do so later if things didn't improve.

I used extra caution crossing streams, and when we took the left fork toward Mount Avalon, I chugged slowly along, stopping frequently. The higher we climbed, the more snow there was. A lone set of footprints frozen in place from the day before led the way over the white rocks. Each of our rest stops lasted a little longer. Atticus, just ahead and above, watched me closely.

The prospect of turning back was becoming more realistic, but I hated the idea of driving five hours in a day and not hiking. I bargained with the weakness within. It wanted a complete stop; I wanted something out of the day. Back and forth the debate went until a settlement was reached. If I could make it, I'd stop at Avalon and call it a day.

Avalon's along the way to Mount Field, but because it is smaller, even though it reportedly had a stunning view, Atticus and I had never stopped there. We always pushed on for the higher peaks. The mysterious illness made each step more difficult than the last.

Atticus was patient. He always was when we were on the trail, taking his ground methodically, then standing and waiting for me. The only time he would return to me was if I took off my pack and sat down.

On a steep stretch, I stretched out my arms and stabbed my trekking poles into the snow. I hung my swimming head between my arms and fought off the dizziness.

When I looked up, Atticus was above me with something dangling from his mouth. It looked like a small gray mitten. But upon a closer look, the mitten was moving while my hiking partner sat above me with an ordinary look, as if he had nothing hanging from his mouth whatsoever.

When I caught up to him, I noticed it was a vole.

"That's not cool. That's someone's life you have hanging from your mouth. Remember to be gentle, please." He looked at me and then let the rodent fall to the snow.

Atticus was never much of a hunter. Well, let me rephrase that. He was never much of a catcher. He loved chasing squirrels but had little luck in catching them. He did get hold of a youngster once, but when I said, "Please, leave it be," he let his quarry go. It scampered away while he looked on in what I imagined was disbelief, first at the freed squirrel, then at me. On another occasion, while we were walking in Newburyport's South End, a small bird had evidently fallen from its nest and was hopping along the sidewalk. He scooped it up into his mouth, and it disappeared. When I folded my arms and lifted an eyebrow, he opened his mouth and the young bird hopped out. It was unharmed. After a quick shake, the bird was on its way again, hopping down the sidewalk.

The vole was lying in the snow, struggling for its life. It writhed slowly on its back, its mouth open, its legs spread out and slowly kicking.

Sadness came over me. As I watched this tiny creature struggling, I forgot how poorly I felt.

I pulled on a heavy winter Gore-Tex mitt and held the vole in my palm. It was dying. I sat down in the snow and Atticus sat next to me looking on. He pressed his body next to mine to get even closer. There we sat, me holding the dying vole, him looking on and listening to me talk about reverence.

Find a quiet trail and you think about all kinds of things. And since it was almost always just Atticus and me on a trail together, my mind often wandered, memories floated back, internal dialogue sometimes became external. There's a lot of good therapy to be found on a mountainside. Probably the best kind.

I was thinking of the woebegone nursing home, and one particular troubled resident, a wretched man. His name was Fred Welch.

He was wheelchair bound by a stroke and decades of drinking. Long ago, his wife and children grew tired of his alcoholism. She told him it was either them or the bottle. Fred chose the bottle.

His family hadn't seen him in years and didn't want to know anything about him other than to be notified when he died.

Fred didn't have a friend in the world. His only enjoyment came in making other people miserable. He did this by swearing at anyone who came near him. The women on the staff were regular targets whenever they tried to help him.

One day I made inroads with Fred by telling him a lie. I walked into his room as if he wasn't there and cussed repeatedly. I turned to him and told him my wife and kids were nothing but trouble. I threw a towel, kicked the trash can, and raged against the injustice of my wife telling me she would leave and take the kids if I didn't stop drinking. He watched rigidly from his wheelchair while I ranted. "Screw her! Screw all of them! Damn kids! I'm going to keep drinking and they can leave if they want to!"

With great effort, he shifted in his chair and mumbled something. I ignored him. He mumbled it again. When I stopped and asked him what he said, he repeated himself, haltingly. "Don't do it. Biggest mistake of my life."

From that point on I had a new friend, and lonely Fred changed. He was more patient with the other residents and kinder to the staff. He'd wait outside his room for me to come down the hall. We talked daily, and each day he talked more. As he opened up, I asked him about his life. I'd ask him all kinds of things.

"Fred, tell me three of your favorite things in the world. List them for me."

He chewed his lip. Then he said, "Watching Ted Williams play baseball. Sophia Loren. Blow jobs."

He smiled.

A week later I asked him, "Fred, tell me something. What are you most afraid of?"

He didn't think long, which meant it was something he thought about. He worked the words up his throat and into his mouth. "Dying alone."

On the day Fred took a turn for the worse and it was clear he was going to die, he was sent to Anna Jaques Hospital in Newburyport. They called it "care and comfort" at the nursing home. A way to make someone's last hours more peaceful, I suppose.

His family was called. They said to call back when he was dead.

I stopped at home on the way to the hospital and picked up a change of clothes and a copy of John Updike's essay on Ted Williams's last at-bat in Fenway Park.

When I arrived, he was already in a private room. Although he was weak, we talked. Mostly, though, I read to him or just sat with him.

The hours ticked slowly by. I held up water with a straw for him to sip from. I wiped his brow with a cool, damp washcloth. When he could no longer sip, I wet his lips with another washcloth soaked in ice water.

After ten hours, he was very close to the end. Neither of us had said anything for a long while, but I wanted him to know he was not dying alone. I sat next to him on the bed and held him and spoke just loud enough for him to hear, "Fred, do you know what heaven is like?"

He lay silent.

I put my mouth to his ear, "Heaven, Fred, is sitting at Fenway Park, watching Ted Williams at bat while Sophia Loren gives you a blow job."

He smiled one last time.

Over the next hour, I watched his breathing slow. I could hear the death rattle. He inhaled less and less. I felt his body release into my arms when life left him.

I showed up so that Fred wouldn't have to die alone.

Throughout the night I comforted him, read to him, held him. When he passed from this world to wherever he was headed, he seemed at peace. Yet somehow, after all of that, I feel I was the one who received the gift.

I learned something that night: if childbirth is a miracle, so is death.

That's what I was thinking of while watching the little vole dying in my hand.

I was distressed that Atticus had taken the life from this little creature, and felt the least I could do was to make sure it didn't have to die alone in the snow. So I held it until I felt the life leave its body.

Just off the trail I scooped a handful of snow and made a dish. I took an extra sock from of my pack and made a bed for the tiny creature by wrapping him softly in the cloth. I laid him down in the indentation.

I did this just in case I had misread it and he was just in shock. Perhaps he would be fine, although I doubted it.

Atticus and I left him and made our way through knee-deep snow on the spur path to Avalon's summit. I had a difficult time in spots where the slippery rocks were hidden by snow and underlying ice. At the summit, I was stopped in my tracks by the magnificence of the Presidential Range covered in snow.

We sat in the warm sunshine, drank in the views, and ate an early lunch. I took photos and wrote a quick letter to my dad, as I did on many of our hikes.

On the way down, Atticus was the first to reach the spot where we'd left the vole. He sat next to the little bed and waited for me. It was dead.

In *Reverence: Renewing a Forgotten Virtue*, Paul Woodruff

wrote, "Reverence is the capacity of awe in the face of the transcendent." He also wrote, "Death is one of the most awe-inspiring facts of our lives."

Perhaps Woodruff's words were one of the reasons I took the time on that day when I wasn't feeling well to take branches and greens to make the dead vole a nest. When I left that nest under an evergreen tree, I paraphrased two lines from John Irving's *Cider House Rules,* substituting "New Hampshire" for "Maine": "Good night, you Princes of New Hampshire, you Kings of New England."

A friend in Newburyport found this story silly.

"It was only a rodent," he said.

To me it was about more than a rodent. It was about these astounding mountains. It was about remembering to say thank you, about showing respect for a place and the lives, no matter how small, that call it home. It was about reverence. I am continually learning about myself and nature, continually remembering what I have forgotten or what I have failed to keep significant in my life. In my journeys alone with Atticus, I'd always found myself being a better person than I'd taken the time to be before.

One day the following spring, on a climb up Mount Pemigewasset before the mountain had turned green, I nearly stepped on a tiny vole. In midstride I noticed him and stopped. Atticus and I sat down to watch him. I pulled a piece of cheese from my lunch and offered a morsel to the vole. He sat up on his hind legs, grabbed the corner with the tiniest front hands I had ever seen, and held on as he chewed.

We sat together for a while. When I shifted my weight, I moved too quickly and the vole ran away from me. He ran toward Atticus and sat between his front legs. Atti looked down at him, studying him calmly, and that's how dog and vole sat until we left.

Our lessons never end. We teach ourselves, and we teach others, and the favor is returned as we become students.

I have no doubt that this enchanted forest and these mountains have made both Atticus and me gentler. Whenever the task of making Will gentle seemed impossible, I'd think about how the forest had helped me. I hoped the mystique would find a way into his tired spirit. As would kindness and respect, and attempting to apply the same golden rule I used with Atticus, by treating him as I would want to be treated if the roles were reversed.

Looking back on the years of hiking before Will came, perhaps I was making myself gentle. I was setting up a home for him when the day came that he arrived.

As our friend Ann Stampfer said, "The mountains, and these woods, are the perfect metaphor for everything else. They prepared me for whatever I would ever face, and allowed me to handle the most challenging things with perspective."

5

Pine Mountain

Nature can show us the way home, the way out
of the prison of our own minds.
—ECKHART TOLLE, *About Nature*

Long before the settlers arrived, the Abenaki Indians knew
the mystique of this land. They considered it sacred, especially Agiocochook, home of the Great Spirit, which they
are said to have avoided. Today Agiocochook is called Mount
Washington, home of a weather station, a cog railway, an auto
road, and a summit cafeteria where you can buy chili, pizza,
hot dogs, and soda.

Most indications that this land was once the home of the
Abenaki are gone, but a few names remain to remind us. No-

table chiefs such as Passaconaway, Chocorua, Kancamagus, Wonalancet, and Paugus have mountains named after them. All are part of the Sandwich Range, which stretches across the southern border of the White Mountain National Forest, running east to west. It is a quieter range than most of the others in the national forest, and the mountains are not as tall as many of the more popular peaks. It's one of the reasons I like the Sandwich Range and accompanying Sandwich Wilderness. The majority of the trails are not as busy. The area is less sexy for those looking for photo opportunities and Instagram posts. But the range's subtlety is exactly what draws me in.

Of all the mountains we've climbed over the past ten years, I would guess we've stood on the summits of more in the Sandwich Range than any of the other ranges.

Another reason I like it, besides the solitude, is that with Abenaki names sprinkled across this area, I feel more connected with those who first knew the land and held it in the highest regard. I like to imagine that when Atticus and I hiked one of these peaks, we were back in a simpler, purer time when one these great leaders ruled their tribe.

I often bow my head when remembering their way of respecting this land. The deified hills, the sacrosanct rivers, the hallowed valleys. It's land that's good for the soul. It fills you up, brings you back to basics, reminds you who you are beneath the layers of ego. Deep in the quietest forests, you come face-to-face with yourself.

Of all those romantic Abenaki names, my favorite is Passaconaway. It translates to "Son of the Bear." New Hampshire legend had it that when the influential Passaconaway, greatest of all the chiefs, died, a sled pulled by wolves flew him to the top of Agiocochook.

The reverence the Abenaki had for this grand enchanted forest touches me deeply and reminds me how privileged we are to live here and to hike through the forests they walked. And whenever I look up at Mount Washington, I can't help but think of the late Passaconaway's mythic flight.

I'm sure this is not the type of Catholic boy Father Merchant and Father Flynn thought they were sharing the Eucharist with back at St. Joseph's in Medway, Massachusetts. I don't doubt that if they were around today they'd echo some of my Christian friends: "You're confusing the creation with the creator."

"It's one and the same," I tell them, and they get angry and want to debate. But what's to debate? They have their beliefs, and I have mine.

On Pine Mountain, which is twenty miles up the road from our home and a hair north of the Presidential Range, there stands a large, primitive wooden cross on an adjoining rise called Chapel Rock. Atticus and I were there one morning when a minister climbed to where we were seated and asked if he could join us. While we were enjoying the panoramic view down into Pinkham Notch, he looked at me, then at the cross. He nodded, "Profound, isn't it?"

"The landscape? Yes."

"I meant the cross."

"I find it redundant."

That led to a pleasing discussion about spirituality that lasted for over an hour. It was refreshing to talk to a man of the cloth who had an open mind and wasn't threatened by other points of view.

I opened my backpack, took out a small notebook, and read to him from my scratchy handwriting: "'We worshipped

Jesus instead of following him on his path. We made Jesus into a mere religion instead of a journey toward union with God and everything else. The shift made us into a religion of "belonging and believing" instead of a religion of transformation.'"

"Who wrote that?"

"Father Richard Rohr."

"Ah, I'm a fan too. He's great."

"I find he takes the sharp edges off being a Christian."

"Are you a Christian?" he asked.

"I don't even think my friends or family know this about me, but while raised as a Catholic, I haven't been to church in years. Yet right before I turned thirty, I considered becoming a priest. I'm fascinated by the soul."

"Why didn't you?" he asked.

"I love women too much. I've also been known to weave together a string of swears freely, even when I pray, and I suppose most important, I don't like church."

We laughed easily. I liked this fellow. "Yes, I think the not-liking-church thing would be problematic."

But that's what is grand about what is known as the "Land of Many Uses." There's room for all kinds of activities, along with motivations and goals. A person can pray to any name he or she wishes to, but also move as silently as a prayer along the trails, stopping to marvel at rock formations, hanging moss, trees twisted into mutant characters, purifying streams, and views from the heaven under our feet to the heaven above our heads.

What I find in these mountains is transformation. As one season sheds its skin to make way for the next, I have

Atticus doing Atticus things as he surveys
Pinkham Notch from Pine Mountain.

An impossibility becomes a reality
when Will reaches a mountaintop.

Will looking upon legendary Mount Chocorua, wrapped in his red coat to keep the winter chill at bay.

A changed Will, free of his harness, cavorting in the backyard during his second summer in Jackson.

"ALWAYS

REMEMBER

THAT YOU ARE

ABSOLUTELY

UNIQUE. JUST

LIKE EVERYONE

ELSE."

———————————

MARGARET MEAD

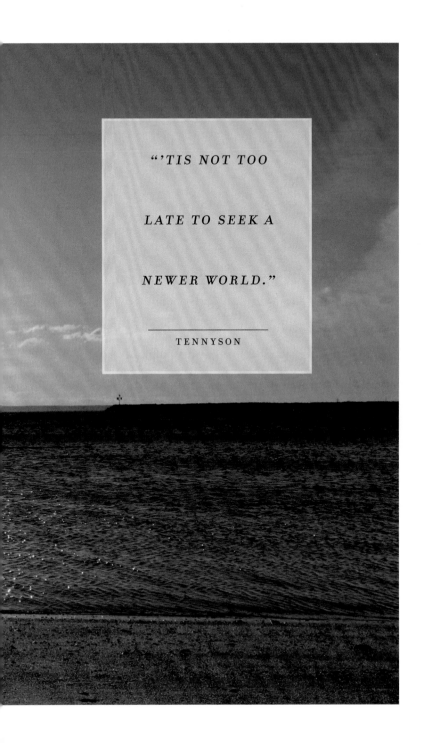

"'TIS NOT TOO

LATE TO SEEK A

NEWER WORLD."

———————————

TENNYSON

Will learns that on the other side of surrender lies trust.

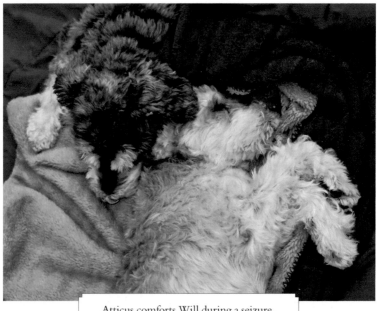

Atticus comforts Will during a seizure.

felt myself doing the same, although my changes come at a snail's pace when they do. No longer in any hurry, or with much to prove, I plod on, remembering it's the passage that counts and not the destination. You could say that spirituality is a lot like hiking.

At the woebegone nursing home, I knew it was the last stop for the residents on their way to death. Not an hour passed there when I didn't contemplate this. While cleaning up the residents, helping them exercise, and assisting them in getting through each day was important, I used to wonder if they were ready to say good-bye. That's why I talked to them about the things I did. I wanted to know their memories, their regrets and victories, their fears, and whatever it was they believed in. Whatever they chose to say was fine by me. I was curious about them, and I also believed it was a gift to have lonely people have someone actually listening to them. Day after day I put myself in their place, felt their loss, and lived their memories.

The nursing home didn't make it a priority for the residents to prepare to die with dignity and peace. Many of the residents were already dead, or at least they weren't really living. Too often I found them sitting in their urine or feces, isolated in their dim rooms with food crusted on their clothes and faces. Women would sit staring out a window for hours at a time in a trance of loneliness. Men would be just as still, often in the dark, with stubble and dandruff and threadbare clothes. Theirs was a still life, an empty and forgotten life.

So much for transformation. For all that they had survived to get to that point in life, no one was there to take note or to celebrate their years.

My short time in that sad facility prepared me for Will. My

role was to assist him to get wherever it was he was supposed to go. I wanted him to know peace and dignity and not have to die alone sprawled out on a cold, sterile table in a strange vet's office.

This was in stark contrast to the way I looked at Atticus. I mean, you don't take an eight-week-old puppy into your life with thoughts of death, but with a fellow like Will, broken and lost and close to the end, that's what I was doing.

But Will was throwing me a curve ball.

His temper still simmered beneath the surface, but as the weeks passed, it seemed to bury itself deeper and deeper. He would still lash out at me, so I continued to exercise caution with him and was prepared for his anger, but he didn't attack as often as he used to. Will hadn't reached where I had hoped he'd get to, but at least he was on the right path.

He was steadily gaining weight and strength, and he was learning to understand kindness. I noticed that he looked at me more, paying close attention as I placed the speakers by his bed or carefully covered him with a towel when he lay down to nap.

In the yard, Will continued to study the tiniest weeds. He'd not only study them, looking at the buds from only an inch away, but also smell them intently. His sense of smell, after all, was his strongest remaining way of appreciating the world. But I also noticed him watch me go about my chores of raking or mowing the lawn. There were even a few occasions when he wanted to play. He wanted to chase me when I ruffled his ears on my way by him, but he wasn't able to walk in a straight line, so he'd kick his legs out and do his best to follow me. I'd wait for him, always talking into his deaf ears, never caring that he couldn't hear me. At least at this point I knew he could see me, however cloudy I may have appeared to him.

On those days when we did play in the backyard, after bouncing brokenly along for about twenty yards in a zigzag pattern, he'd need a break. When he stretched out on the grass, I sat next to him. Always he watched me.

Some days I felt like he was trying to figure me out, like I was one of his little wildflowers that he loved to pay attention to.

It helped that I was learning how to touch him, to let him see my hand move toward him from below and not from above or behind where he couldn't see it. Rarely did I touch his hips; mostly it was under his chin, then up along the side of his shoulders to his back and the top of his head.

Whenever I had touched his hips, even gently while trying to reposition him or pick him up, he'd snap at me. I added a dose of Metacam to his food to help with the pain relief at the suggestion of Christine O'Connell. I was cautious about using it, because I'd heard that prolonged use wasn't good for his digestive system, but who knew how long he had? And I didn't want him to be held back by pain.

We may have taken him in to give him a place to die, but on the way to death, Will appeared to have other plans. I grew curious as to how long he'd last, and how far he'd go with his reclamation of his life.

That first summer was filled with good news, but at Christine O'Connell's office one afternoon, she shared some bad news with me.

"I have something to tell you."

I waited.

"I'm leaving North Country Animal Hospital."

Christine was one of the reasons I decided to take Will on. I knew she'd be with us every step of the way. I didn't tell her that, and I wasn't resentful that she was moving on, but I found myself suddenly lurching, unsure of my footing.

She was headed south to Exeter, New Hampshire, not far from Newburyport. I was already calculating how far we'd have to drive to keep her as our vet. We were already driving down to Boston to see Atticus's cardiologist a couple of times a year to keep track of his benign heart murmur, so we were used to traveling.

Losing Christine was like losing a member of our family, but she urged me to try another doctor at the practice. A couple of minutes later Dr. Rachael Kleidon came into the room with Christine. She seemed nervous, excited, a bit giggly, but nice. She was tall, and Christine was shorter. Those contrasts should have been enough, but there were other differences. It wasn't just Rachael's laughter; it was how they handled things. Christine was grounded, had an edge and strong instincts to go straight at a problem. Rachael was subtler, sweetly polite, and methodical. Because Christine believed in her, and I believed in Christine, I decided we'd try using Rachael as our vet and see how things worked out.

But during the car ride home to Jackson, I was mourning the loss of someone special in our lives, who had been part of our story.

During the first week of August, *Following Atticus* came out in paperback, and a tour had been organized for Atticus and me. We were to drive to various independent bookstores throughout New England. We'd be on the road for about a week to kick things off before returning home. The remaining events would take place more sporadically.

With the help of Laura Cummings, the owner of White Birch Books, and Virginia Moore, the director of the Conway Area Humane Society, we used the launch as a fund-raiser for animals in need. It took place at North Conway's Red Jacket Mountain View Resort, and a posh dinner was served. There was an exuberant crowd on hand. Will was with us and in grand form. He was happier than I'd ever seen him. As was his custom, out in public he was closer to me and considered me a confederate more than he did at home. We were fast friends in that busy room.

Before the dinner and my talk, I carried him around the room while Atticus walked with us. Many in attendance had read about Will and seen his photos on our Facebook page, and they were eager to meet him.

Our friend Leigh Grady made sure Will went outside for breaks as often as she could, and once, when Atticus and I had him outside, we saw a fox striding across the lawn before stopping to observe us. I took it as a good sign to have another wild visitor that close to us, and I kissed the top of Will's head.

"Hey, buddy, looks like one of your friends came by to say hello."

When Leigh didn't have him outside, Will was free to walk around the ballroom. I was standing on the makeshift stage, with Atticus seated on a table next to me. We watched Will meander throughout the room. I was distracted by his apparent joy, the way he fit into the setting, his confidence, his curiosity. Hands reached out to stroke him, hoping he'd stay for a visit. There was this ease to him, and the hitch in his gait was hardly noticeable. There was no head tilt, and he held himself proudly. He was healthy and strong, and moved like he belonged there.

He walked to the stage and looked up at me. His vision was believed to work at maybe 50 percent, but the moment I came into sight, he recognized me and his demeanor became bouncier. His eyes were bright and round. Watching me gesture and speak, he seemed to glow. When I picked him up and introduced him to the crowd, he leaned his head against my chest, and when I told them his story, I could feel the room fill with love for him. It may have been the launch of our paperback, but it had turned into Will's coming-out party.

Early the next morning Atticus and I left Will with Leigh as we set off on our little book tour. He couldn't have been in much better hands. Leigh's life was a succession of good deeds, including visiting Harvest Hills Animal Shelter to walk the dogs who were waiting for homes. She doted on Will, took him to work with her and to the local gardens where she tended to her vegetables, and saw to his every need.

Out on tour, I called to ask her how he was acting, and I was told he was fine. Secretly, though, I wondered whether he felt abandoned again.

I had wanted to take him on the road with us, but it would have been too much for him because book tours are filled with excitement and interaction, and they are also exhausting. It's one of the reasons I was grateful our publisher understood the relationship between Atticus and me and created a tour that catered to our needs. Instead of flying to cities around the country, which Atticus would hate, we took our car. We stayed in the Northeast, and by the time each event was over, we were drained. Driving to events allowed us to seek out nature along the way. We stopped often for walks, and by the time we were at our next appearance, we would show up fully recharged. All of that would have been too much for old Will.

At the end of the week, we arrived at Leigh's work to pick up Will. While Atticus ran to say hello to Leigh, I walked around the counter to find a very different dog.

It was Will, but not like I'd seen him before. He rushed up to me, his eyes even bigger and brighter than the night of the launch. His front paws were bouncing up and down repeatedly, wanting me to hold him. He was breathless. I swept him up in my arms, and for the first time since I knew him I heard him whimper. Not a sad, terrible kind of whimper, but one of relief and happiness. He nuzzled against my neck, and he couldn't contain his excitement. He kept singing his little song for me, his heart racing against my hand, his head pushing farther against me to get even closer. I squeezed him tight and rocked him back and forth, back and forth. When he grew silent, I kissed him on his nose, something I wouldn't have done before for fear of his teeth. That's when I heard his snores.

Back in Jackson, Will became more interactive. He followed me around our home. Outside, he'd prance along, making sure I couldn't get too far away. His front legs were so expressive, so optimistic, the way they kicked out like he was a spirited horse, but his hind legs continued to hold him back. What was missing in mobility he made up for in celebration.

In the days to come, whenever Will napped and Atticus and I snuck out for a while, we'd come home to find Will aware of us. If he was in the bedroom, his head poked around the corner like a child hoping to see Santa on Christmas Eve, and he'd come trundling out to greet me.

As fall arrived, I rejoiced that Will would spend a third season in the mountains. The little dog who came home with us to die was instead ready to enjoy New England in her autumn finery.

It had been an active summer in our yard. I'd never seen our wild neighbors in such numbers before. The Jackson Five, a mother bear with four cubs, came by several times, and once when they were here I noticed that Aragorn had come back again too. He was behind the brush in the vacant property next to us. His body was thicker, his coat shinier, but he was still young and ungainly. When the mother and her four cubs left, Aragorn stayed behind, watching the three of us in the yard. I was on my knees with Will, and I noted Atticus watching Aragorn from his usual Will-free patch just below the trees. It wasn't the last time I saw the young bear spying on us from behind the trees that fall.

On one of the last afternoons we saw Aragorn, I received a surprise when we were back inside. Will was still eating, but not all at once any longer. He would nibble at this food, walk away, come back for more. Instead of giving him three meals a day, I simply filled his bowl at the beginning of each day. I had been putting his Metacam in his food. But since his eating habits changed, I began using a syringe to inject it into treats. To keep the peace, I offered Atticus a snack on his perch on the couch first. When I turned around to give Will his medicine, he was looking up at me with a puppy's gaze, a delightful look of expectation on his face. There was something else too. Something I couldn't quite figure out. I stood up straight and looked down at him again. That's when it hit me. Will was sitting!

Often we overlook the smallest things while craving the

bigger rewards. But Will's progress was a reason for gratitude. And it wasn't just sitting; it was nearly everything. With Will, small steps were reason for big celebrations. For him to have nothing, to have lived so long without health and happiness, and to see good things return to him one at a time was like stumbling upon little gifts around our home. To be part of it, to be witness to it, was humbling. Grand things were happening!

When I'd learned Will was coming to live with us, I fantasized about getting him to a mountaintop. I hoped he would have a chance to experience what Atticus and I had done more than a thousand times before. Paige Foster used to see the photographs of Atticus sitting Buddha-like and gazing off into the distance, and she'd say proudly, "He's doing his soul work."

That's what I wanted for Will. I wanted him to have the opportunity to feed his soul with some of our vivid scenery. Unfortunately, as soon as I met him, I realized there would be no mountaintop hikes for him.

Four days before we picked up Will, I wrote in my journal about the goal of bringing him up Black Cap Mountain in North Conway. It's an easy hike that Atticus and I used as a morning walk on some days when we weren't hiking. In just over a mile, the elevation gain is only 650 feet. That's about as easy as it gets in these parts. I wasn't sure if he would be able to walk it or not, but I figured I could always carry him.

Unfortunately, as soon as I met him, I knew he couldn't be carried up Black Cap. His body was a wreck, and those back legs didn't work. He couldn't manage walking the short, flat Jackson loop, never mind a small mountain. He'd fight with me if I tried to carry him. No, my original hopes for him were dashed.

However, as the months passed and Will grew healthier, I revisited the possibility. We stopped by Eastern Mountain Sports to see how he'd like riding in one of the child-carrying backpacks. He happily let me pick him up, but when I slid him down into the seat, he started to cry. There was too much pressure on his hips. I tried him with his legs tucked under him and with his legs dangling out of the holes. Either way he was in too much pain. Every few weeks, as his strength and health returned, I'd try again, but the results never changed.

With the snows of winter not far away, the chances of getting Will to a mountaintop were less likely with each week that passed. On top of that, I wasn't sure he would make it through the harshest season. Snow falls heavily here, and when it begins, it's here to stay. The backyard gets buried in three feet of snow during a typical winter, and it remains until spring. Will wouldn't be able to get his exercise. He'd have to settle for moving about in our driveway to stay active. If I didn't get him up a mountain soon, I never would.

In early November, I had an idea. I thought of Pine Mountain. The approach is along a dirt road closed to vehicles. And from that road to the summit is only half a mile of easier hiking. I went online and ordered an all-terrain pet stroller from Pet Gear. It came on a Saturday, and I put Will in it for the first time. He seemed to be comfortable, and without further ado, the plan was set for the following day.

One of my hiking friends, Cindy Netska, agreed to help.

I had no idea if Will would enjoy it or not, or whether we'd even be able to get him to the top of Pine Mountain, but I wanted to try. If things didn't go well, we'd turn back.

It seemed easy enough on paper. The round trip was less than four miles, most of it along the dirt road. But the road was steeper than I remembered. Atticus did what Atticus does, leading the way, and Cindy and I took turns pushing the Will Wagon uphill, sweating and gasping for oxygen as we went. Will was content to ride along; he hadn't a care in the world. I put several blankets in the stroller for him, but he slipped out of them and spent most of the trip sitting up, watching through the half-zipped mesh screen (fully zipped, the screen caused Will to panic, because I think it reminded him of a crate).

After pushing up the dirt road for more than a mile, we reached the trail. Before going up, I took Will out in a small area of grass to give him a break. His legs may not have brought him that far, but they were taking him all around the field. He hopped and turned, bounced, even began to trot. He was making up for his ride by strutting. In the background, massive Mount Madison stood watching over him while he played.

I've walked up that spur trail many times before and many times since, and it's always been very easy—except when the Will Wagon was involved. At first Cindy and I tried to push it up the trail, but it was jarring and we didn't make much headway. The rocks were too large for the wheels. Finally, we decided to carry it like a sedan chair.

Cindy lifted the front, and I took most of the weight in the rear. We didn't make it very far before stopping. We were tripping on the rocks and roots and sliding in the mud. We moved ten, twenty, maybe thirty feet forward at a time, and had to stop for a rest. It was a laborious process. When we'd stop, we'd breathe deep for air and feel the burn in our muscles. But we'd do it again. Another ten or thirty feet. Another rest. I started to doubt we'd make it. We were so close, but

I've never been so tired climbing a mountain. Usually I felt a climb in my legs, my back, my heart and lungs, but to feel the burn and exhaustion in my upper body on this trek doubled the difficulty. My arms began to shake, my biceps cramped. I wasn't sure how much farther we could go, yet we'd come that far. I didn't want to stop. Repeatedly we carried Will forward, rested, and carried him some more.

When we finally reached the top, we were spent, but I was so excited that my strength returned. Atticus hopped up on a viewing rock and I took Will out of his wagon and held him up to look at the views across the valley to the Carter-Moriah Range, the summit ritual I'd always done with Atticus. We'd climb to the top together and take in the views on our own before he'd walk over and poke me in the leg with his nose. When I held him in the crook of my elbow, Atticus always sat as still as a statue. There was quiet, a sense of peace. Before long, and I learned to wait for it, he'd settle his weight into my arm and against my body. Then I'd hear it—a deliberate sigh. Always a sigh. No mountain trek was complete without it.

I had wondered what Will would do if we ever reached a mountaintop. Would he be able to see much through cloudy eyes? Would that weak neck betray him and leave his head flopped to one side, waiting for me to prop it up?

When I picked him up and rested his bottom inside my elbow, I placed my other hand on his chest to steady him. Within a second, there was stillness. Whenever I picked Will up, he'd look at me. But not on Pine Mountain. His eyes cast about. I watched him looking at the view: the mountains, the valley, the river beyond. He seemed to study it, and I didn't have to hold up his head.

I waited and hoped and waited some more. I felt it begin.

Air left his chest. He relaxed his body against mine. I felt his belly relax. Then came a little sigh, and Will relaxed even more, giving me all of his weight.

Soul work.

Six months after moving to the mountains, Will was on top of one.

My eyes were filled with emotion. I was so proud of him and how far he'd come. Everything we had gone through together in the prior months was worth it at that moment. It was everything I'd hoped it would be.

His head began to wobble. He rested it against mine. At the same time we turned to look at each other, and that's when I felt another first. It was as feathered as angel's wings, as faint as the gentlest breeze. Will kissed me.

It was a day of firsts, but it wouldn't be complete without sitting down next to Atticus, who was seated on a large rock, looking out at the view and watching Will and me. Sitting with Will in my arms on my right side, I felt Atticus lean against me on the left. I thanked him for being kind to Will, sharing his home with him, sharing me with him, and now, sharing a mountain with Will.

That night, we were all tired. Blissfully so. I told Ken and Ann about our victory and they were jubilant. Marijane and I talked about Will's progress and our mountain success. Our Facebook page, which now had around ten thousand people following the everyday adventures of Atticus, Will, and the fellow they lived with, erupted in celebration at the news of Will's mountain summit.

The expedition to Pine Mountain was the end of six months of anger. Will's rage had dissipated over the previous several months; his temper tantrums had nearly ceased, but not completely. From that moment on, though, they did. Never again would he try to bite me or anyone else.

No matter what we were to encounter after Pine Mountain, I knew we'd reached a treasured place, and that proved to be the best medicine for Will. Christine O'Connell had been right all along: old age is not a disease. For Will, it was a fresh start.

6

The Cough

True love begins when nothing is looked for in
return.

—ANTOINE DE SAINT-EXUPÉRY

December's snow fell fat around the black ash tree and
filled up the backyard. The winds roared down from
Pinkham Notch up north like a freight train. They shook the
house when they rumbled by overhead. Icy fingers pried and
tapped at frosted windows. Through it all, Will slept contentedly beneath the Christmas tree. Its scent was divine to
him. He'd spend nearly the entire day in that corner of our
apartment.

I had witnessed his fondness for wildflowers, how he'd often lie down with them and inhale their blossoms through the fairer months. When they stopped growing, I began to buy flowers for him each week, hoping it would make him happy, and apparently it did. For whenever I'd place them next to him, he'd smell them, and often sleep next to a bouquet if I left it on the floor.

That's the reason the tree went up right after Thanksgiving, because I knew he'd appreciate its wild scent, and I wanted him to enjoy it as long as possible. I'd find him sniffing the pine boughs, and the shiny red, gold, and green ornaments captured his attention when they reflected the twinkling lights. Christmas carols filled our home, and they were delivered by vibration to Will. So did the aroma of homemade muffins baking in the oven and of hot soup in the ever-present slow cooker. The tiny flames of candles flickered, and cinnamon and peppermint mingled with other kitchen smells. With the cold outside and the warmth of the inside, there is no better word to describe it than *home*.

In our cozy little hobbit hole, life was good.

Atticus and I continued to take advantage of Will's lengthy naps. We ventured out for our regular walks through the winter scenes at Echo Lake and did shorter hikes around the valley to low peaks with expansive views. No matter how frozen the landscape, how biting the wind, this was Atticus's season. The older he got, the less he enjoyed the heat of summer. But when the mercury dropped and a nip could be felt in the air, Atticus seemed younger, bouncier. Unlike when he was younger and we were both getting used to the coldest months in the mountains, he no longer needed his body suit to keep warm. He had grown used to the season.

The big surprise was that when I brought Will outside to

our snowy driveway to frolic for as long as he would enjoy it, Will was at ease. He had shivered through the mornings of May and early June, but now he was robust, weighing seven pounds more. Other than his adorably strange gait and his interpretive dance that combined half-spinning, drunken waltzing, a fractured gallop, and half leaps, one wouldn't be able to tell there was anything wrong with Will. Even his eyes appeared to focus more. He was no longer lost, nor did he look it.

We visited the stores that welcomed him so he would get more exercise, for he couldn't push through the deep snow in the yard. We stopped often at White Birch Books, and Will was now as self-assured there as Atticus had always been. He'd roam the space nonchalantly, and people who didn't know him would say hello, not realizing he was deaf, and he'd walk by them. With others he'd stop, tilt his head in their direction, and take note of them. After shopping for books, we'd make our way over to Four Your Paws Only, where fresh-from-the-oven cookies were always waiting in boxes for Atticus and Will from friends on our Facebook page who had called in the orders.

Our backyard was a crystal palace, coated in white. I put another Christmas tree outside on the crown of the yard and wove blue lights through its boughs. I filled the bird feeders and sprinkled extra handfuls of sunflower seeds generously around the trees for the squirrels. I hung the suet feeders by the upstairs windows so we could watch the birds from the couch.

When our friends David and Lisa came north to ski for the first trip of the season, Lisa looked at Will and said, shocked, "That can't be the same dog!"

Six months earlier, when we were down in Newburyport for a night, Lisa had watched Will for a few hours. He became aggressive when she tried to get him back inside the house. But when I picked him up and placed him in her arms during the Christmas holiday, he settled in.

Will grew to love human touch, and being held. At a book event in Winchester, Massachusetts, our friend Laura Bachofner—who first brought Will to my attention by posting his story on our Facebook page—was in attendance. Right before the event started, I brought Will to her and she held him for the next ninety minutes. When it was time to leave, I don't think she wanted to let him go.

Will's only remaining issue was that he continued to go to the bathroom inside the house. That wasn't going to change. The night accidents were the worst. I'd be deep asleep and somewhere far away I'd hear his cries. They were panicked and pitiful, high-pitched yelps for help. Those were the many nights of the two-o'clock-in-the-morning baths. That's when my sleep deprivation started.

There were other nights when he woke me up because he had gone for a nocturnal walkabout and found himself stuck in a corner or wedged in some tight cubbyhole, for Will was always exploring and forever getting stuck. He couldn't back up and he'd stay where he was waiting for me to pick him up.

As our time together progressed, I slowly learned a few tricks, including spreading towels on wooden floors and in the bathroom. I began filling in all the spaces he'd find himself trapped in. I blocked them with large plastic bottles of detergent or cleaning fluid, or turned chairs sideways and laid them on the floor. I placed a piece of plywood across the doorway to the extra bedroom, which served as my writing room, so he couldn't pee on the carpet. I was Will-proofing our home as I learned more about him.

It feels strange to write about urine and feces so easily. But live with either long enough, love the one you are with, and even piss and shit become an acceptable part of life. One night I heard Will crying. I bounded out of bed and planted my foot in a pile of shit. There was nothing else to do but laugh—and hop to the bathtub on one leg.

Since I was no longer getting a full night's sleep, I started taking naps with Will early each afternoon. Atticus joined us, but made certain that I was between the two of them. Because I worried about Will falling off the bed, these naps always took place on the floor.

Atticus was forever patient with Will, giving him his space and some respect, but after Will's first few months of misbehaving, Atticus would never be his buddy. Not that Atticus was ever any other dog's friend. He was kind to them and intrigued by them, just as he was with moose and bears and fox, but with dogs it never lasted more than a few minutes.

Early each morning, Atticus sat on his corner of the couch and I'd sit on mine, half turned so I could look out the picture window to a wall of nature. Will's ritual was to approach me, waiting to be picked up. If I didn't respond quickly enough, he'd bump my leg with his nose. I'd lift him onto my lap and hold his head up with mine, and together we'd look out the window. I knew that Will could make out shadows and shapes and light, but I'm not sure how detailed his vision was beyond that. There really was no way of knowing. Sometimes he picked up on the movement of the larger birds. Having the snow across everything provided some contrast in the scene for him and made it easier to see some of the movements he'd miss in summer. Even with his limitations, though, he'd study squirrels going about their business and birds flying from tree to tree or landing on a nearby feeder. He would move his head; his eyes would focus and follow the movement. There was something of a child's expectation of magic in his eyes during these little morning get-togethers. But it never took him long before his head would nod. He'd be watching attentively, and within ten seconds his eyes would blink and close and he'd be sleeping.

I'd lay him on his bed on the floor and cover him. I never left him on the couch, for fear he'd fall off and break something. And if I placed him in the middle of the couch when I was sitting there, Atticus would hop off and go to his own dog bed.

It was clear that in Atticus's mind there were places Will was allowed and those he wasn't. The bed and the couch were always Atti's islands of refuge from the smelly, stumbling white dog.

Since that morning long ago when Atticus had found Will beneath my side of the bed, after he crawled over to me during his experience with the old dog vestibular disease, he never bothered acknowledging Will.

God bless Will. I think he finally grew tired of being ignored. One morning, while we were getting ready to go out, Atticus sat facing the door. Will walked up to him and circled around. Atticus kept looking straight ahead. Will drew closer and closer still as he circled. Finally he stood within inches of Atticus's left ear and let loose with one loud, resounding bark. Atti didn't flinch. Even then he wouldn't acknowledge Will.

That bark was so piercing and strange to hear that I laughed. "He's telling you, 'Pay attention to me, Atticus!'"

That was the only time I ever heard a bark in our home. Atticus was always silent, and other than his fits of aggression with me and his frantic cries while feeling trapped, Will was forevermore also silent.

The first area rug was long gone. A second took its place. Towels were picked up and washed if they were soiled. I steam-mopped the floor daily and bathed Will a few times a week. In this way, life with Will was like spending time at the woebegone nursing home, where there was a futile battle against the constant underlying smell of urine. But in every other way, it was just the opposite in our little place. Will was reborn of spirit, and hope and happiness had returned. Things couldn't have been better—which only meant we were due for a change.

In January, Will had his first seizure. He was standing up when abruptly he began shaking. His fall came quick and he was splayed out flat on the floor, where he continued to tremble. He was gasping for air, his tongue hanging out of his mouth. His eyes rolled back. I lay next to him and stroked him gently. Atticus approached and watched over him. When Will calmed down, I picked him up and wrapped him in a blanket and we sat on the floor in front of the couch. He slept in my arms that night.

At North Country Animal Hospital, Rachael Kleidon gave Will a thorough checkup. Blood work was done. Nothing significant was found.

The seizure was distressing to me because it was all too reminiscent of Max. That's how his life ended. Seizures came from time to time. A few months later they came and didn't stop. He was suffering so much that I chose to end his misery and say good-bye to him.

I was haunted by that memory and hoped it was a onetime episode. But a week later, a second seizure hit. It lasted a little longer and left Will spent. There was nothing we could do, though, so I waited and hoped they'd stop.

I watched him closely. How could I not wonder if this was the beginning of the end for Will?

Death was whispering to me. "I'm getting closer . . ."

I didn't fear her. Some are surprised when I tell them I find death to be a miracle and a grace. I accept her role in my life, in all of our lives, but that doesn't mean she is incapable of breaking my heart. I am not worried about the day I go. I'll leave like Joseph Campbell said: "You go to your death singing."

What I was struggling with was figuring out when to sing for Will. I'd only have one chance to get it right.

Winter months in Jackson are much more night than day. They are dark everywhere, but in the mountains, the sun sets behind the peaks and the days are even shorter. The evenings are long and frozen, and spring seems an impossibility.

When the seizures didn't return for a few weeks, I decided we could all use a dose of nature and some glorious light. I rented a beach house in Provincetown on the tip of Cape Cod. The Cape is known for its sunlight, especially Provincetown. The land is flat and you can watch the sun rise out of the ocean and set into the bay.

In Provincetown, there are miles of endless beaches with barely anyone around. The town shuts down, except for a handful of stores and restaurants. It's a madhouse in the summer, but in winter, you can walk for miles through the dunes and see only seagulls.

So we were off to the shore, where there was peace, to the Wired Puppy Coffee House on Commercial Street, where dogs are allowed and the lattes are strong, and to a little rental with wooden floors with a stash of paper towels and cleaning supplies.

The goal was always to wrap Will in as much nature as I could, not just so he could see through foggy eyes, but to also feel it—on his skin, drifting over his white hair, and even in his lungs. I wanted him to inhale it and to become part of it, as it would become part of him. I'm not sure what he'd experienced before, but I thought he'd love the ocean air and the sand beneath his paws. Our little studio opened right onto the beach. It was a slice of perfection.

The ocean is cousin to the mountains in New England. Both have a tough primal side, but they inspire. And if the fabric of the natural world could inspire humans, we who have often let the comfort of what we've built rob us of what connects us to nature, I imagined Will would find it invigorating.

That first night, we sat on the chilly sand under mild air and watched the stars. Atticus and I were warm enough, but because we weren't moving I wrapped Will in a blanket and held him on my lap. We stayed outside until my eyelids grew heavy, and for the first time in months, the three of us slept straight through until morning.

We woke when the sun lifted itself out of the water. Outside, Will started a little drunken butterfly dance to greet the day. He trilled with excitement at the water's edge. The sand was cool against his paws and he bounced and frolicked, welcoming distinctive smells and a new adventure.

There was a dusting of snow on the outer Cape and the bike path was clear, other than the drifting beach sand. Because it was winter and no one was using the beach, we ignored the "No Dogs Allowed" signs. What's a little civil disobedience among friends, especially when there was soul work to be done? Atticus and I took Will out in the Will Wagon, utterly bundled up so that only his face was showing. We walked for miles, stopping every half hour for Will to get out for some exercise. When we arrived at Race Point, the sky was clear enough to hurt my eyes, and all three of us squinted. Gusts of wind buffeted us, even blowing Will down, but he'd get right back up again. Waves crashed nearby and sea spray coated us as we walked along the water's edge, with sea-foam reaching up to greet us. We saw no one on our walk, and Atticus ran up and along the dunes to where the sea grass started to smell where other dogs, and coyotes, had left messages.

I tried to stop Will from walking into the water, but when he managed to do so, I wrapped him up and dried his feet with a towel, then put him down again.

When the seagulls screeched, I think he heard them. I'd only ever see him turn his head like that once before, when one of the blue jays in our backyard was letting out her high-pitched cry. He cocked his head, as if to say, *Give me more,* and the seagulls did. If they were close, he'd walk by them, and when they flew off, he'd jog his crooked line, sprightly with mischief. It was the only time I saw him pay attention to another creature other than Atticus. Other creatures were always watching him, sometimes close enough to even touch him, but he never noticed them or responded.

We ended another day under the cover of night, pushing the Will Wagon through the ghostly empty streets of Provincetown under the glow of streetlamps. But back behind our cottage, we could see the stars so clearly.

When the full moon took center stage, I held Will up to see it. I don't doubt that he did. In the middle of that darkness sat a huge glowing orb, climbing slowly. Looking at him next to me and seeing the moon reflected in his eyes, his mouth slightly open, all I could think was that as Will aged, he was becoming younger.

Whenever there was a new texture or smell or sight to behold, I wanted him to take in every bit of it. Knowing he'd likely been kept captive in a crate, I wanted him to be free. That's the week he started his newest phase: life without a harness, collar, or leash. Not that I ever used a leash with him, since he was always by my side.

From that time on, he was as naked and free as Atticus was.

On our fourth day we woke up to snow showers. The sky was a brooding charcoal, and the water a lighter gray and as smooth as glass. A layer of snow settled on the sand, except where the lazy ebb and flow washed it away. Wayward snowflakes drifted down around us. It wasn't like the snow back home. It was tender and the temperatures were mild. Will and Atticus explored the area as I sat with my camera, recording Will's time with the sea.

In that serene place, in the midst of that quietude, I heard Will gag. He turned his head. He gagged again. Throatier this time. His body went into spasm when he coughed. Then he stopped coughing, and he was choking, fighting for air. Fighting to breathe.

I ran to him. But Atticus, who was closer, reached him first. He stood in front of Will and gently pushed his nose against Will's.

In midstruggle, Will's squinting eyes opened, and so did his mouth. He gulped in some air. Atticus stayed with him, touching his nose one more time. They looked into each other's eyes until Will's breathing became calm and steady. I fought the urge to pick him up. Instead I watched them facing each other.

A white dog and a black-and-white dog looking deep into each other. Behind them, the sky and sea were slate gray. In front of them, the ground was white with snow. Silence returned. The water whispered as it drew up to the sand and eased back. The snowflakes came now, true snowflakes, big and fat. They settled on us, and around us.

A seagull flew overhead, it cried out, and Atticus walked away, along the water's edge. Will followed him until he could no longer keep up. That's when I picked up Will and carried him through the miracle of falling snow. Together we followed Atticus down the beach and the flakes gathered on my shoulders and in my hair, and some found resting places on Will's long black eyelashes.

We stayed in Provincetown for two more days and walked and napped and played. But the two dogs remained separate after they had touched noses on the beach. I'd find Will looking at Atticus, but Atticus never returned his gaze. He was back to keeping Will at a distance.

From the beach house I called Marijane in Arizona. She hadn't been to Provincetown in decades, and it was so different from her home in the desert that she wanted me to describe everything we'd seen, and how the salt in the air and the sea spray felt like on my skin. She asked about Will.

"I wonder if he has ever been to the ocean before. Does he act like he's enjoying it?"

I didn't leave anything out, including how deeply we slept through the nights. When the subject of Will's choking came up, I could tell she was tensing up like she was there watching it. But when I brought up Atticus's cure for Will's breathing issues, she seemed to understand. I could feel her relaxing. Her time with the Navajo and their legends had broadened Marijane's view of the world. The young nun who had never been more than an hour out of Boston had become a mistress of the mystical.

She once said, "Tommy, the Church was a good place for me to start, but there were other plans for me, and I ended up where I was supposed to be, learning what I was supposed to learn."

Before we hung up, she asked me if I would put the phone up against Atticus's ear.

"I want to say something to him."

He was sitting up on the couch, looking at me. When I went over to him I said, "Marijane has something she wants to say to you."

He looked at the phone and I held it up to one of his ears. I could barely hear her murmured voice and with her words his ears and eyebrows rose and lowered, rose and lowered.

When I thought she was done, I asked, "What did you say to him? He seemed very intent on this side."

"I shared a Navajo blessing with him."

"Really? What was it?"

"That's Atticus's story to tell. If he wants to share it with you, that's up to him. Good-bye, Tommy. Walk in beauty."

Just for the record, Atticus has never shared what Marijane said to him that day. I added it to all the other secrets he kept.

Will's seizures didn't end, but they seldom came after that, and because they were less intense, I no longer worried about them as much. I'm not sure exactly why that was. Perhaps something was born in me during those weeks that taught me not to worry about things I couldn't do anything about. Or I realized that each day holds its own challenges, and when they came along, somehow I'd be ready for whatever it was. And then there was strange, otherworldly Atticus. It seemed that he knew a thing or two I didn't. I have never been closer with another soul in my life, but it would be silly to pretend to know the mysteries he carried through life.

Living with Will was living on a razor's edge. On one side was life, on the other death. But when I checked in on how I was feeling about when I'd one day have to say good-bye to Will, I realized it would come when the time was right. Maybe I did my mourning for Will when I first met him and he was only half alive.

When I was much younger I went on a date with a psychology student, and she gave me a fun four-question quiz. I answered the questions and she took notes. She later told me that my answers to the questions revealed my feelings about how I saw myself, how I thought others saw me, how I felt about sex, and last, a fourth subject.

The last question was "You wake up in a pitch-black hallway. The only reason you know it is a hallway is that you can put your hands out and feel the walls. You begin to walk. Slowly you make your way along. There is no noise other than your footsteps. You walk and you walk and you walk. You walk for ten minutes, thirty, maybe an hour, always in the darkness. Ultimately, you come to a door in all that blackness. It's at the end of the long hallway. The only reason you know it's a door is because you can feel it. You blindly search for a doorknob, find it, turn it, and . . . it is locked. What's your initial emotion?"

She looked at me like I was strange when I answered, "I'm excited!"

"What?"

"I'm excited. I want to know what's on the other side."

"That's weird . . . Most people say they are frightened or panicked or anxious. No one says they are excited."

"I did. What's it supposed to mean?"

"It's supposed to reflect how you'll feel when you die."

That made sense to me. I do want to know what's next.

In our unassuming life of meeting each day as it came, I no longer stressed about how a city councilor was going to vote, if a developer was going to tear down a historic building and put up one twice as big in the same small space, or if a bad cop was going to get reprimanded for stealing evidence or stalking women in his cruiser.

I have Max to thank for making me care about something more important, Atticus for helping me truly believe in our infinitude, the forest and the mountains for stripping me down and building me back up again, and finally, Will, for teaching me humility and acceptance.

There is humility in dedicating yourself to another. In serving others. In a way, washing the feces from Will's fur, or holding him through a seizure, or seeing him awaken to wonder again—every bit of it was humbling. All of it seemed like some kind form of atonement, and I began to take comfort even in the unpleasant tasks.

I used to worry so much about changing my family when I was young, or Newburyport when I was older, but I was learning that the best way to change this world is to change yourself and your perception of it.

W̶e woke up to a mild morning on our last day on the Cape. It was still dark out. The stars to the west were hung with care, and they looked down on us when we went outside to await the sun. The eastern sky went from dark to gray, and when a flicker of flame sparked the horizon it was like someone spilled orange paint on the heavens and it was spreading up. When the sun appeared it was enormous and the water and the atmosphere burned pink. Atticus and I sat next to each other, and Will skipped in his distinctive way to the sun. The higher it climbed, the stiller he stayed. When it was all the way out of the water, he tilted his head as the blinding reflection reached across the ocean to meet him. He pulsated and tensed, and ducked his body as well as he could. When he was at his lowest, he sprang up in slow motion and tried to leap. His front legs danced in front of him while his rear legs stayed where they were, planted on the sand. Three times he kicked his legs out as far as he could, and then he turned in our direction. I walked over to him and he readied his body for me to heft him up. In my arms, he sat in the crook of my right elbow. We looked at the sun together, just as we had looked out at the horizon a few months earlier from the ledges of Pine Mountain.

"Will, I'm glad you liked the ocean. Maybe we will come back again next winter. What do you say?"

In response he tucked his head against my neck.

An Uninvited Guest

Not till we are lost, in other words not till we
have lost the world, do we begin to find
ourselves, and realize where we are and the
infinite extent of our relations.
—HENRY DAVID THOREAU

A question can change a life. It can inspire us, send us in
a new direction, and wake up a tired heart. A question
can have lasting effects that send ripples out across the world.
Goodness knows I asked Will questions all the time—not that
he could hear any of them.

"Could you please show me who you are?"

"Can't you see I'm trying to help you?"

"How do I make the pain go away?"

The question that changed Will's life, however, didn't come from me.

Four simple words. They were enough to start a movement. You wouldn't think something so small would have lasting consequences. Then again, we're talking fairy tales here.

"Are these for Will?"

"I'm sorry?"

"Are the flowers for Will, or are they for you?"

"They're for Will, but what difference does that make?"

"When they're for Will, I pick out more fragrant flowers. When they're for you, I choose flowers that are nice to look at."

That in a nutshell is the magic of Dutch Bloemen Winkel. The Dutch "Flower Shop" is a Jackson surprise. As charming as our covered bridges, country inns, and the little white church are, it's a tiny flower shop in the center of the village that has the most charm. All year long, but especially in the fairer seasons, brides-to-be from across New England descend on the small shop to order flowers for their weddings. Jackson is a favorite place for those who are getting married. The scenery is straight out of a postcard. The inns are something out of old movies set in New England. Weddings in our little town are all the rage.

The morning I went in to buy flowers for Will, Carrie Scribner, the owner, wasn't there, but Orly, one of her employees, was. Like most of the people Carrie employs at her shop, Orly has a rare kindness about her and is a fitting extension of Carrie. Not that Orly isn't special on her own, but I think that Carrie's kindness rubs off on people.

Carrie is like Monsieur Perdu in the novel *The Little Paris Bookshop,* a self-proclaimed "apothecary of books," but *her* specialty is knowing just the right flowers to prescribe for a spirit in need of a lift.

On top of being an artist, Carrie is one of the kindest people I've ever met. With her husband, Joe, their young son, Grey Bern, and Tulip and Toad, two black French bulldogs, they have created their own magic in their rustic home on the side of a mountain. When I chose to sidestep drama in my life and avoid those who drain others, I also made an active choice to spend time with people who embrace life. So while Carrie's flowers were always striking, the woman behind them was equally so, as was her friendship. All one has to do is walk in the door of the shop to feel special.

I have come to like the civility of flowers in a home and appreciate the feminine burst of nature. They add elegance to our modest life. You may not find much hanging on our walls, but the bookshelves are full, and the vases are islands of loveliness.

A town is right for me when there is an honest mechanic, a good bookshop, an empathetic vet, and an intuitive florist. In Jackson, we had Dutch Bloemen Winkel and the Wildcat Service Station, while White Birch Books and Rachael Kleidon were near enough in North Conway. There wasn't much else I needed.

In a simple arrangement of flowers, Will found the entire universe. He needed little else to raise him up and take him somewhere else. They were his drug of choice, whether he was out in the yard, responding to the call of every unknown wildflower and aromatic weed, or inside, admiring a mason jar full of life.

So I decided to plant my first garden that spring. It was a small patch of wildflowers, only three feet by ten. Will watched me as I used a pitchfork to turn the soil, raked it free of weeds and rocks, and dropped to my knees to plant the seeds. The package promised a mixture of flowers, and I wasn't sure what would come up, except at the far end, where I also planted pumpkins.

Pumpkins ripening in late summer and early autumn feel like New England to me. Like flowers for Will, they simply make me happy. Since living in Jackson, I always put out pumpkins, not only for me, but for the wildlife to nibble on at night.

The garden served three purposes: flowers for Will; pumpkins for the bears, raccoons, skunks, and me; and something for the butterflies and bees.

When Will looked at me on all fours, my hands rich with soil, I said to him, "This is for you, Wildflower Will. Your own garden."

We watched the daily progress. First came little green shoots, and then the buds shyly showed their faces, before a full bloom surprised us one morning. They were small but hopeful. Others came up taller, even looking like weeds, but pretty nonetheless. Will didn't care what they looked like; he cared what they smelled like. As the garden matured, I'd find him pushing his way into the middle of it to sit and look around. I'd find him sleeping among the blooms many an afternoon.

I wrote about Orly's question on my blog and Facebook page, which, like Will's garden, had blossomed, from six thousand followers the year before to fourteen thousand. On any given day, thousands of people would check our page the first thing in the morning. They wanted to know what Atticus was up to, and they were overjoyed by Will's redemption. I thought it was a sweet story to share, unaware of the seeds I was sowing.

The following day, Carrie called to say that flowers were sent to Will by a woman in Colorado. A love note was attached. The day after, Carrie received a call from a woman in South Carolina. Her arrangement came with a note celebrating Will's life and fondness for flowers. That was just the beginning.

Week after week, the arrangements kept coming for Will from across the country. The calls were so steady that Carrie suggested to those ordering that the deliveries should be staggered. I don't doubt she may have lost some business this way by telling folks intent on showing Will how they felt about him that she already had three orders for him that week. Month after month, Will was buoyed by the generosity of his admirers.

The pictures I took of him with his flowers showed Will's resurgence. His eyes reflected a spirit reclaimed, those long lashes so becoming, a look of peace and belonging on his face. And of course there was the way he glowed while appraising the latest bunch of love to come in. It was contagious. People from across the country saw what the flowers were doing for him, and wanted to add to his pleasure. And I found out from their comments on our Facebook page that people were not only sending Will flowers; they were also buying them for themselves and those they loved. If I could give the little dog I lived with flowers, they reasoned, they could do the same for people they cared about, and the dogs and cats they lived with.

Others took more time to notice the dogs they lived with, and reported if they also enjoyed wildflowers. And it didn't stop with flowers; people told me they started to think more about what pleased the dogs and cats in their lives, other than chew sticks and catnip.

Will's love of music and affection for flowers were having a rippling impact on the lives of other animals.

With the return of the warm weather, the Will Wagon became a fixture around the Jackson loop. People greeted Atticus, who would often give them a little leap as he passed, as if saying hello. And Will was meeting many for the first time as he rode contentedly along. We'd often stop to visit with Kevin and Michele Pratt at Flossie's General Store, just through the covered bridge. I'd let Will out, he'd cavort on their lawn, and each time we visited with them, I could see Michele's crush on him grow.

Will had that impact on people. He was lovable and suddenly embraceable. There was something about him that glowed. It was especially noticeable to those who had followed his story from the beginning of his time with us. They'd seen what he was, and witnessed what he was becoming.

"Is it okay if I give him a hug?" they'd ask.

"He would like nothing more."

The dog who had trusted no one now embraced being embraced, leaning in as he was pulled into the chest of an admirer.

Sometimes on these walks I'd see Aragorn on the other side of the street. Although he was growing, he was still more mischief than stateliness. I could see it in the way he dodged through the trees or the fields, like a young boy following a parade through the center of town.

One evening I saw him in front of Flossie's when it was just Atticus and me. He was on the porch, checking out the old-fashioned Coca-Cola cooler. When several cars pulled up to take his photograph, he bounded across the street but quickly stopped halfway across the far lane, directly in front of a car. He turned to look at us. Fortunately, the car saw him coming and stopped.

Atticus walked ahead of me, and I waved to Aragorn. "Good evening, Aragorn."

Thirty minutes later, when we had returned home, I went upstairs and carried Will into the yard. Aragorn was watching us from the edge of the trees. At first he stood on all fours, then up on his hind legs, as if to get a better view, and then he dropped down to watch us.

That little bear was filling out and looked halfway to being an adult. By the time he was fully grown, I guessed he'd weigh three hundred pounds. That's if the hunters didn't get him first, which I always prayed they wouldn't.

For now, though, Aragorn was part of our little community of personalities. He contributed to the life we were living in that little patch of the possible halfway to wild. For there is little in this world more fantastic than to be living your life, only to see one of nature's wildest beasts walk across your yard. No matter how many times the bears crossed on their way to town—and sometimes it could be weeks in between, or only hours—my heart would leap and I would realize how very fortunate we were to live in this place.

As much as we saw various bears, and some enough to give names to, Aragorn was distinctive. While the other bears came and went, he sought us out. From the first day he followed us home, he seemed interested in us. He had adopted us the same way we'd adopted him.

All of it added to Will's magical kingdom. While Atticus enjoyed the freedom of his enchanted forest—the entire White Mountain National Forest—the backyard was Will's, with his wildflower garden, the surrounding trees, the melodies of birds, and the hum of bees. Even our lawn was enough to make Will happy. He'd be stopped in his walks by a lone dandelion. He'd lean in and study it, and sometimes he'd look at it so long that he'd slump down when he became tired, and fall asleep under the weed's spell.

If Atticus was more like John Muir or Henry David Thoreau, feeling a kinship to the wild, Will was our Emily Dickinson, the world revealing itself to him in the confines close to home.

Will was so busy living, and I was so busy tending to him, that I almost forgot to celebrate his one-year anniversary in Jackson. Our friend Roy Prescott remembered, though. Roy hosts the early-morning show on WMWV 93.5 in North Conway. He invited us into the studio to talk about Will's first year. When Will's Facebook fans found out, they tuned in to the live stream in such vast numbers that it overrode the station's capabilities. At the end of the interview, Roy asked me what song I wanted to dedicate to Will.

"'I'm Alive' by Michael Franti."

From then on, this was considered Will's song, and Will's friends tell me that when they hear that jubilant tune, they can't help but think of his prancing and dancing.

That night, as we settled in, with even more flowers than usual around us, I thought of where Will had come from and where he now was as I raised the blanket halfway up his shoulders to keep him warm in his slumber.

We had much to be grateful for.

P erhaps that's why I didn't worry all that much when Atticus started to limp in the mornings. I thought he might have caught a toenail on the carpet when jumping off the couch. Or maybe he had tweaked a joint or a muscle on a recent hike. He was still able to do our regular walks through the village, and the hobble disappeared as the day wore on. He and I had always experienced minor aches and pains through the years due to hiking, and this one didn't seem any different.

When it didn't improve, we went to see Rachael Kleidon. "Just to be certain," Rachael took an X-ray of Atticus's foot. Everything was fine, but there was a small infection around a nail bed. She prescribed some antibiotics and I cleaned the nail regularly.

It improved. And then it worsened. Within a couple of weeks, he couldn't walk on it. When I examined his paw, I found a swollen and bloody toe.

When I first heard the term "osteosarcoma," every fear I've ever had overwhelmed me, but I held on, knowing it was only a possibility. But when Atticus was taken in for another round of X-rays, and I had to wait in the hallway, I retreated to get some fresh air. Outside, my legs grew weak, and I leaned up against my car. I tried to swallow my fears. I don't think that anyone hears "cancer" and doesn't immediately feel nauseous and light-headed.

I called Ken and Ann Stampfer. They were our best friends, and there wasn't much we didn't share.

When Ann answered the phone, I couldn't form the simplest words.

"Hello?"

I felt dizzy.

"Hello?"

I spit out something about Atticus and bone cancer and I struggled without being able to say much. I had to hang up, telling Ann, "I'll call you back in a few minutes."

Who knows what raced through their minds in the twenty minutes it took me to call them back. The fates of the four of us had been woven together through all the miles we shared walking up and down mountains.

I took a couple more minutes outside and told myself to get strong, and to do it quick. This was about Atticus, not me. I inhaled, gathered myself together, and after my few minutes of fear, I resolved to get ready for whatever was coming.

The X-rays revealed that a bone in one of Atticus's toes was disappearing.

When Rachael and I spoke, she was tender and kind. Her concern was clear in her voice, and it was for both Atticus and me. Rachael Kleidon understands the relationship of the animals she cares for and the people they live with better than most. When she told me the toe had to be amputated, I was pragmatic about it.

"Okay. It's not like he can use it like it is. But will he be able to walk okay?"

"Yes! I think he'll be fine. Dogs make a full recovery from this kind of surgery. But we're going to send it off for a biopsy to see if there's cancer."

I had concerns. Ever since I followed Paige Foster's advice to carry Atticus as a puppy wherever we went, Atticus and I

were inseparable. There wasn't anything we'd didn't face together and do together. The flip side of that intimacy was that
Atticus didn't do as well when we weren't together. He was
not as self-assured in those moments, not calm. He'd panic on
the rarest of occasions when we were away from each other as
he tried to figure out how to get back to me, for he felt that I
was his responsibility in the same way I felt he was mine.

The next concern was what to do if it was cancer. There
was the cost, for one thing. I didn't have much in my bank
account, and I wasn't sure how I would be able to pay for an
operation.

Rachael told me not to worry about the finances. I could
pay for it later, no matter how long it took.

And if it was cancer? "Well, Tom, there are some options we
can talk about, but let's not worry about that until we have to."

My tendency is to plan for the worst and hope for the best.
"But you think it's cancer, don't you?"

She hesitated until she looked like she was the one diag-
nosed with it, and she said, "Yes, I think it is, but we'll have
to see."

I was still concerned about being separated from Atticus
when he needed me most, so Rachael asked for a few minutes.
After talking to the staff, she made an offer to do something
the hospital had never done. She invited me to sit in on the
surgery.

Lovely, kind, compassionate Rachael. Not many doctors
would make that offer.

Surgery was set for the following week. Atticus's paw was
cleaned and wrapped heavily. She prescribed painkillers and
antibiotics and we headed home. As I looked over at him in
the passenger seat, Atticus was sitting the way he always did.

The wrap on his paw didn't seem to concern him. On the way, we drove through the countryside and along the Saco River, while he enjoyed the views.

I carried Atticus up the stairs, and when I opened the door, there was a puddle of urine in the middle of the floor. It was a reminder that realities are always there. A puddle of piss. Amputation. Cancer. How could I not laugh?

Will poked his head around the corner and trotted out to greet me while I was on all fours cleaning up the puddle.

When I carried both of them down into Will's backyard kingdom, I said, "Atticus, if you die before Will, I'm going to kill you!" When I laughed, Will could tell I was in a good mood, and he wanted to play. Meanwhile, Atticus sat off to the side in his stoic way, watching how silly the two of us were.

Yes, I was in a good mood, in spite of the circumstances. This is what friendship is made for. It was for climbing mountains and sharing the view and facing troubles together. You don't get one without the other. Worrying wasn't going to do any good. It would only get in the way of any good energy I had to offer Atticus. So why waste time with it?

I guess I stopped being a worrier when Atticus came along, and through the years I returned to the woodland realm I had feared for so long. There was a time I was addicted to drama. I'd leap at any reason to get upset, and I'd focus on what was wrong. My metamorphosis can be traced to surrendering to the forest, the challenging climbs, and our move north and my desire to live in a simpler manner.

Facing the amputation of Atticus's toe, I realized I had finally turned the corner and learned the art of acceptance. I joked with Ken and Ann, saying, "If there is a word that sums up my life at this time, it's 'monastic.'"

In spite of my oft-colorful language, I was feeling monkish. There was Atticus and Will; there were books on philosophy, theology, and poetry; there was music; and of course there was nature.

I was also affected by my relationship with Marijane. She lived so far away, but we talked several times a week, and our conversations were as long as marathons. We had gone decades without knowing much about each other, but after my father died, we fell into each other's life and there were no secrets between us. How strange it was to know her for my entire life, but not truly know her. We relished our new bond, which seemed timeless. We started many conversations talking about the weather reports in New Hampshire and Arizona, but then we'd bound into flight and carry each other away in a torrent of conversation.

She was impressed when I introduced her to Joseph Campbell's writing, particularly because they shared an appreciation of Carl Jung. And I was impressed when she suggested we read James Hillman's *The Soul's Code* at the same time and call each other to talk about it. After Hillman, I suggested Don Miguel Ruiz. She countered with Eckhart Tolle.

Jack Ryan's youngest sibling and his youngest son kept him alive with the stories we shared about him. His role in her life was unfamiliar to me, while she knew very little about what kind of father he was. Dad and Marijane had talked often, but he had never revealed the depression and anger he struggled with. Of course he wouldn't share that with her. She was still the little girl who looked up to him when he went off to fight in World War II. He pampered her throughout her life, often sending her money or other gifts. Jack Ryan cared for all of his brothers and sisters, but Marijane was his favorite.

What Jack wouldn't have cared for were the books we were reading. Oh, he may have when he was a young man and was hungry to prove himself to the world, but as the decades passed and his dreams faded, he settled into reading every mystery in the local library. He craved the adventurous life he once dreamed of having.

After Tolle, I suggested to Marijane that we read Mary Oliver. We'd take time reading her poems to each other. Once, twice, often three times—one of us would read a selection out loud as the other read along silently. The poems touched on grace and nature and animals, subjects the two of us were passionate about.

I didn't get as much out of Michael Singer's *The Untethered Soul* as she did. But when she introduced me to Richard Rohr's books, my horizons expanded. For a man who was not religious, but forever fascinated by souls and the flight of the spirit, Rohr was an approachable Franciscan. He doesn't preach in his books; they feel as if he and I are sitting down to have tea together. From the moment I read his belief that "Nature itself is God's first, oldest, and clearest scripture," he won me over.

My conversations with Marijane and our discussions in our two-person reading club contributed to my evolution, and my monastic life.

When Marijane wrote to ask if I was nervous about the possibility of Atticus's having cancer, I wrote, "I'm ready for whatever happens. I have learned to have faith through the years that he and I have immersed ourselves in the forest and stood atop innumerable summits. We've faced nearly every challenge the world can throw at us. I feel confident we'll face this one just as boldly."

Then I quoted *Learning to Walk in the Dark* by Barbara Brown Taylor, describing how my life had changed on the trails, "The only real difference between anxiety and excitement was my willingness to let go of fear."

Truly, what was there to fear after all?

For forty years I had stumbled through life looking for my rightful place. When Atticus came along as an eight-week-old puppy, somehow we figured things out together. I had discovered something I was good at—being half of Tom and Atticus. We had done things the right way. Our lives were enhanced by each other.

Still I prayed. Boy, did I ever. I prayed so much that God probably said to an angel, "Take a message, it's *him* again." (No, I don't really believe that.) I put the words of hope and faith out there and reminded myself that we had a great doctor to work with us, and Atticus and I were fighters.

New friends we'd made in the mountains reached out to us, as did those we'd left behind in Newburyport. But the most fervent support came from thousands of people on our Following Atticus Facebook page, people we may never meet.

Everybody was worried about us, and some thought my calm was a sign of denial.

To me this is the grace that is offered when things like cancer are knocking on your door. You are invited to come to the realization that you can't do anything about what has brought you to this place in time, but you can determine how you'll face it going forward.

In the days before the surgery, I carried Atticus and his

splinted leg into the woods, or to the Saco or Ellis rivers, or Jackson Falls, or by Will's wildflower garden and pumpkin patch under the stars in our Adirondack chairs, and I'd repeat various versions of the same prayer.

"Thank you. Thank you for this friendship. Thank you for everything. Thank you for letting us go through this together. Thank you for Rachael Kleidon."

Before I had been welcomed home by the forest and Atticus and I forged a new relationship along mountain trails, I would have played the part of a victim. Why me? Why did Atticus have to go through this? But in the face of this threat, I made the choice to concentrate on what we had instead of what we didn't. I told Marijane that's how I knew I was growing up, finally, in my early fifties: I was learning the importance of gratitude.

"Besides," I reasoned to friends, "if anyone should have to struggle through cancer, isn't it better that it's us? Seriously, everything we've ever been through has been about facing things together and head-on. So why not us?"

I'd like to think my faith was fueled by love and experience. Atticus and I loved each other, and years of rugged mountain experiences formed the patches of the quilt that represented our shared life. We no longer hiked the great distances, nor did I feel the need to be as intense, but once you rush into the wind on top of Mount Moosilauke, or step into the abyss of a cloud bank along the Bondcliff Trail above the tree line, you take that experience with you forever. Moments of vigor and adrenaline contribute to your fortitude. All we had faced readied us for all we would encounter, and allowed me to say, "Fuck fear!"

In a way, there I was in that four-question psychology quiz

from thirty years earlier. I was in a long dark hallway, treading carefully along, feeling my way in the pitch-black, until at last I'd reached that locked door.

The prospect of cancer, I told myself, was just another mountaintop. Step by step, we'd scale it to see what was on the other side.

We had each other, and we had Rachael. That was more than enough. And if it wasn't, well—fuck fear!

R achael telephoned the next day. She was weeping. Her voice was breaking when we greeted each other.

"Rach, what is it?"

"It's, um . . ."

"Is it the blood work? Did you already get the results? Is it bad?"

"No, it's . . . um . . . it's . . ."

"It's what?"

"It's all so beautiful!" In a burst of words and tears and light laughter, she said, "It's amazing."

"What is?"

"You know how you posted about what's going on with Atticus on your blog yesterday?"

"Yes?"

"The phone hasn't stopped ringing here. People have been making donations toward your bill. It's just beautiful!"

I hadn't mentioned anything about money on our blog. I wrote about facing up to our fears and getting ready for whatever was to come. I wrote of the amputation and the possibility of cancer. Donations as large as $500 came in, and as little as $5 (sent from a woman in Maine who had to get by on a disability check). In twenty-four hours, $7,000 came in, and when Deb and Jaime, the receptionists, told them they had enough money for the bill, people asked to be put on waiting lists.

"Let us know if they need more."

The surgery went well. I didn't want to get in the way of Rachael and her staff, but when Atticus was stretched out and she was removing the aggrieved toe, she kept calling me forward to be as close to him as possible. I placed a hand on him, hoping he'd sense me while under anesthesia. Maybe not in a cognitive way, but in that ethereal bond that connects us to those we love.

The severed toe was a mass of bone, blood, soft tissue, and tumor. It didn't turn my stomach. It didn't do anything to me. I was thankful it was gone, and I knew that soon he'd be able to walk without a splint, and then without a limp. All that was left was to await the results of the biopsy.

Fuck fear.

I was with Atticus when he woke up in the little recovery room. There was a cast on his leg and each of the employees at North Country Animal Hospital signed their names on red felt hearts and stuck them to the wrap. He was drowsy when he opened his eyes, and the first thing he saw was me, which is what Rachael and I wanted. Several blankets were draped over him, and his head was on my hand, which was on a pillow. He looked worn but calm.

He didn't try to move, he merely gazed into my eyes. I

stroked his head, running his floppy ears through my fingers, and I spoke softly to him.

Text messages were lined up on my phone. The front desk was receiving e-mails wishing us well, and wanting to know if there was any news. Virginia Moore, the director of the Conway Area Humane Society, stopped by to say hello to Atticus and to give me a hug. Flowers were delivered to the hospital for us, as were dog treats. Others bouquets were awaiting us on our deck at home. At the center of this buzz was the still point. At the still point we sat together.

When the anesthesia started to let go of Atticus, I carried him out back. I placed him on the ground and he stumbled about with his long, stiff cast. He was groggy and in some pain, but he hopped farther than I expected him to, ending up in the middle of the sprawling lawn. Eventually he sat down. When I approached him, I realized he was looking through an opening in the trees across the valley to the mountains of the Green Hill Preserve: Black Cap, Cranmore, Peaked, and Middle. Little Buddha had found his mountains even on the day they took a portion of him away.

Will was never curious about Atticus's paw or his cast. I'm not sure he had the ability; all his energies seemed to go into living for the next minute. But he was happy when I brought in all the flowers from Carrie's shop that had been left on the deck, and he hopped up and down when he saw them.

Christina Morse, one of the moderators on our Facebook page, sent me a recording from the WMWV morning show in which Roy Prescott sent out heartfelt good wishes to his friend Atticus M. Finch, his voice breaking with emotion. Thanks to Roy, many in the Mount Washington Valley were rooting for Atticus.

We didn't have to wait long for the results. Rachael described them so even I could understand.

"It really is very good news that it is not bone cancer and that we got it all. So we can all be very happy right now. The biopsy results came back as squamous cell carcinoma, arising from the nail bed of the second digit. It has low metastatic potential, so it's not likely to spread, and there are clean margins."

When we hugged and celebrated the results, she added, "I can't believe the support throughout all of this. I continue to be amazed by the response from so many people all over the world!"

But I soon heard from Rachael again. There were follow-up concerns. "The mitotic index of the cells they looked at is higher than the pathologist is comfortable with. I think we need to talk about our options."

The options were to ignore it and hope the cancer wasn't spreading elsewhere in Atticus's body or to start chemotherapy. Atticus was eleven. I wasn't sure how I felt about him having poison pumped into his system at his age. I didn't want what could be one of his last years to entail six months of chemotherapy. Besides, getting chemo would mean heading to a bigger hospital in Boston, Portland, or Portsmouth, and they wouldn't bend the rules and allow me to stay with Atticus during treatments.

Once again, I put my belief in our good doctor.

"You know, I could do the chemo here so you and Atti could be together, Tom."

"I didn't know you did chemo treatments here."

"We don't. But I'll get the instructions from an oncologist and I'll stay in touch with them the entire time. It's up to you."

When Rachael told me she was concerned about the cancer returning and that she'd move forward with the chemotherapy if it was one of her dogs, I agreed with her.

Twenty-five days after his amputation, Atticus and I stood on top of Black Cap Mountain. It's not a difficult hike, but because it was the first since the surgery, there was reason to celebrate on the summit. He did well, and you would never know he was missing a toe if it wasn't for the strange shape of his paw.

Four years earlier, Atticus and I had stood atop Black Cap for a similar rehabilitation hike. Twenty-eight days after I had emergency gallbladder surgery and survived a near-fatal case of septic shock, Atticus had led me up a mountain again. Now it was my turn to walk with him during his recovery.

With one less toe, he did far better than I had four years prior, hiking with two tubes sticking out of my abdomen, one of which was connected to a large drainage bag.

When I was in the hospital, the staff let Atticus visit me every day. Each night he'd stay with Leigh Grady and her husband, Kevin, which he hated. It was nothing against them, but he thought his place was with me. Early each morning Leigh dropped Atticus off in my room.

I smile when I remember Dr. Bob Tilney walking into my room one day to examine me and finding Atticus lying on the bed while I was in a chair next to him. He looked at Atticus watching me from the bed. "Would it be possible for the patient to get on the bed so I can examine him, please."

It was all good-natured, since Bob was also a dog lover and had seen Atticus and me tramping around the back roads of Jackson by his farm on many occasions.

In the days after my surgery, the septic shock still had hold of me. I was weak and in so much pain I could barely sit up. The first day I was able to walk only ten feet, and I thought I was going to faint. The next day it was twenty feet. Within a few days, though, I was following Atticus around the ward. We plodded along. Twenty laps, then forty, and finally about a hundred. Me with my rear end barely concealed by the hospital gown, and Atticus going as slowly as possible in front of me, constantly checking to make sure I was okay.

The night following Atticus's first chemo treatment was a rough one. He was shivering on the couch. When he went to the door, letting me know he had to go out, he crossed the backyard and disappeared into the high grass. I found him lying down in it, as if he were hiding from the discomfort. I sat down with him and waited until he wanted to come inside again.

The next morning, when I awakened, he stared down at me in bed. His ears were riding low. He was trying to tell me something.

"You okay, Atti? Not feeling well? Come on, let's go outside."

But when I got out of bed, he led me to the kitchen, where he stood next to a pool of diarrhea. It wasn't from Will, because he had slept through the night and was still under his covers.

I thanked Atticus for showing me, shook my head in

amazement, and demonstrated what an expert I had become at cleaning up shit. I was beginning to see the exercise of cleaning up feces and urine as a Zen thing, albeit one I had to breathe through my mouth while doing.

Atti's discomfort didn't last for long. He was feeling better by the end of the day, and he was full of energy the day after that. He was doing so well that the two of us hiked Pine Mountain to watch the sunset. We gazed at a burnt-orange sun sliding toward the horizon from the top of Chapel Rock. In the quiet, I heard a curious sound off in the distance. It sounded like matching lawn mowers. They were drawing steadily closer. I couldn't figure out what it was.

Then two motorized hang gliders appeared. The pilots were sitting in little buggies as they whirred in large circles over Pine Mountain. As they neared Chapel Rock, one of the men yelled down to us.

I couldn't hear what he said and put my hand to my ear. "What did you say? Couldn't make it out!"

He circled back and flew slightly lower. *"I said, is that Atticus?!"*

"Yes!"

"Keep going, Atticus! Kick cancer's butt!"

When they flew out of sight and off into the sunset, we had the mountain to ourselves. As the sun plunged behind the western horizon, it left behind a fiery sky. We hurried over to Pine Mountain, half a mile away, to one of the viewpoints we had taken Will to the previous autumn. A full moon was rising behind Mount Moriah. It was enormous, as full moons are when they're still close to the skyline. Blue turned to dark blue and the black night fell, and we watched the full moon climb along the ridge and glow orange. The way it was riding right up along the mountain, I thought of Sisyphus pushing his giant boulder up the hill, only to have it come down again so he'd have to start anew. I figured that's what the chemo would be like. Atticus would feel weak, get stronger, and then it would be time for the next treatment. Six were scheduled over the next five months.

We sat on a large rock and leaned into each other. I held his water bottle out for him to sip from while I drank from mine.

It had been warm when we started up Pine Mountain, but the air turned that kind of cool that feels like you are almost swimming through it. The scent of the forest rose like perfume, we heard a nearby crash, most likely a moose, and we too became creatures of the night.

"Thank you for everything."

I wasn't just talking to Atticus.

When we lived in Newburyport but drove north every weekend, whenever we'd be out on a trail before sunrise or after sunset, I became nervous. The six-year-old we all have inside us would wake up screaming about being afraid of the dark. Walking through the woods with a headlamp only magnifies that six-year-old's fear. Tree branches become the gnarled hands of witches, and when you turn your head and the tunnel of light catches a glimpse and shadows are thrown, those witches seem to be moving. It didn't matter how often we walked through the darkness. I was always slightly unnerved, imagining the supernatural more than anything else. Bears and moose didn't frighten me; we'd seen them before. Once when a supermoon rose in midwinter, it was so bright out I turned off my headlamp. Atticus and I were on South Doublehead, just a few miles from home. Our nighttime trek was illuminated by the moon above and the reflective snow below. It was like walking through a photographic negative. The mountain slumbered, and the only noise was the slap and bite of my snowshoes and the stab of my trekking poles. While moving toward the saddle that dips between North and South Doublehead, I looked up as we cruised along, and just before walking into him, I saw the huge bull moose walking directly toward us.

"Psst, moose," I whispered to Atti, and he sat down. The moose was now within a few feet of us. In a hushed voice I asked Atticus to get behind me and was cautious with my movements.

All three of us were using the same path cut through the deep snow, and I knew this huge beast was not about to back up. He took another step toward us, and I could smell the musk of him in the clean air. He rose above me. I was ready to pick Atticus up and hop off the trail, even if I would be up to my waist in the snow.

Two more steps forward and we'd bump heads.

I slowly turned toward Atticus behind me. But before I bent over, the bull took another step, but cut left through the drifts toward the east in the saddle, a place where we'd always witnessed moose activity in the past. He slipped away gracefully, a huge ship passing quietly, with soft grunts and long plunging legs.

On that same trail, in close to the same spot, one Fourth of July, we ran into a porcupine. We had taken Leigh Grady up to watch the fireworks. Atticus stayed close to me and we crouched down to watch the porcupine. She turned her back to us, but when we didn't move, she did. She crawled up onto a rock and sat looking at us. It was over in a few minutes, but how exciting it was to see her eyes shine and the tips of her quills illuminated by my headlamp.

Leigh told me, "I'm glad you are in front in case we run into a bear."

"Leigh, not to worry. Most likely, if a bear is going to be aggressive, he'll come from behind."

Poor Leigh, I think she may have spent the next mile or so looking over her shoulder.

On another night, we actually did encounter a bear. It was deep in a long tunnel of trees on the climb up to North Doublehead, and it was standing on its hind legs. I thought he was a man at first, until he dropped down and ran into the dense growth on the side.

No, moose, porcupine, and bear didn't frighten me at night while in the forest. It was more the irrational fears of ghosts and goblins and unnatural things. And every noise that cannot be explained away as part of nature prickles your skin. Many a night I'd find Atticus watching me curiously as I banged my trekking poles together repeatedly and sang off-key songs.

It's strange, though, that when I gave up the *Undertoad* and began to strive toward the light of life, I was no longer afraid of night hikes. I could feel my breath rise and fall with the rhythm of nature. I learned to relish the freedom of slipping away from the comfort of home as night fell and we became just as ghostly as the spirits I once feared.

It seems I had left my anxieties back in the man–made world.

It was in the pitch black of these hikes, in the utter charmed loneliness of late nights, that I realized how special the stars are. Yes, there was darkness, but there were all these points of hope in the heavenly expanse above us.

I didn't realize it at the time, but that night on Pine Mountain was the last hike we'd ever take at night. Atticus's eyes were having a more difficult time in the dark, and of course, there was Will to take care of.

Writing this, I realize how much I miss the many hours we spent walking through the night on a mountain. Eventually, what used to unsettle me—even downright scare me—turned into a communion and affirmation. With some sadness, I wonder if I will ever experience that again. And even if I do, it will be without Atticus, and that brings about an entirely indescribable emptiness to mind.

E ach chemotherapy treatment was harder to recover from than the last. Atticus weakened. Our milder hikes and even our walks grew less frequent.

The sessions themselves were fine. Rachael and I would laugh, and Atticus would relax as she inserted his port and hooked the tube up to it and the syringe up to that. As she slowly sent the poison into his body, he relaxed even more. Each time I'd place my phone against Atticus's side and play Ralph Vaughan Williams's *Fantasia on a Theme by Thomas Tallis*. I would place a free hand under his chin and he'd rest his head on it, look into my eyes, and ease into sleep.

After each session, we'd stick around for ninety minutes, just to make sure Atticus was handling it well. We'd walk in the hospital's large yard and find ourselves seated in the grass taking in the view of the mountains. I'd bring a book of poetry with me and read it out loud as Atticus laid his head against my leg.

Because I continued to tuck Will in almost every night to

music and sometimes shared the videos on Facebook, some of his fans sent blankets to cover him with. They were all hand-made, with "a hug in every stitch," as Betty Teller Fagen from Long Island noted with the one she had knitted.

The first were a couple of prayer shawls from Lisa Money in North Carolina, a cancer survivor and a thriver. One was a deep red, the other blue and white. The note said, "One for Atticus and one for Will." But other than on chemotherapy days, Atticus never needed them. They were all Will's.

Through summer and into autumn, I was grateful for the way people were connecting with Will and Atticus. Will was receiving a steady supply of flowers, and eventually he had close to thirty afghans and prayer shawls.

I was thankful for the blankets for Will. As had happened in his first year with us, Will's skin started breaking down. It became crusty and hard, spreading over his forehead, down his neck, onto his back and across his chest and sides. I kept those areas closely shaved, applying medicated ointments, and gave him daily baths with a special shampoo.

Unlike Atticus, Will enjoyed water. He was a good patient when I kept him in the tub for up to twenty minutes.

During that second autumn with us, I noticed Will was losing weight. It wasn't much, but those blankets made a lot of difference, because for the first time in over a year, he was beginning to shiver again.

At Four Your Paws Only I bought a red coat—handmade in New Hampshire—to keep him warm. It was lined with thick white fleece that also showed around the edges, and it had a thick white Santa Claus collar over his shoulders. It was quite the fashion statement, and as the leaves fell, Will bounced around in the backyard in his new coat looking festive and comfortable. Those following Will's story loved these photos of him, and the staff at Four Your Paws Only was besieged with requests for the red coat Will was wearing. I'm told the woman who made them was a one-person operation, and as a steady stream of orders came in, she'd say, "Don't they want anything but red? I've made all these other colors already." But Will's friends wanted the coat Will wore.

His little red coat became Will's constant companion if it was under seventy degrees. Even during the next spring and summer, if there was a slight breeze, he'd need it for warmth.

This was Will's first sign of decline after a year and a half of improvement.

Will's baths were not only good for his skin, they were therapeutic for his body. I towel-dried him when I took him out of the tub. He'd look at me with such seeming clarity that I'd say to him, "Hey, who are you, and what did you do to the fellow who came from New Jersey?"

I carefully dried his ears, his belly, and each leg. The next step was to put him on an old massage table and warm him with a heating pad. I massaged him, kneading cautiously into his muscles. He now let me work the muscles around his hips, and when I took him through range-of-motion exercises he was tranquil and trusting.

I joke with my friend Martha House, a Toronto artist, that between us we have three degrees.

"What are you talking about?" she said the first time. "I have three degrees!"

"I know, and I flunked out of three colleges when I was young and stupid. So between us we have three degrees."

I may have flunked out, but I'd learned a thing or two. Seeds had been sprinkled that took a while to germinate. At the universities I attended, I majored in exercise physiology, and worked as a student athletic trainer with the sports teams. I studied massage, and finally, after thirty years, what I learned was being put to use. I had worked on seven-foot-tall basketball players and football linemen who weighed three hundred pounds. Now I was massaging twenty-five-pound Will. The technique was the same, except with Will, I didn't press as deeply.

One of the other seeds that fell along the path of my youth was an English literature class I took. I was a lazy student and didn't dedicate myself to my studies. But I remember a teacher talking about *The Canterbury Tales*. Something within me bubbled with excitement, but learning more meant reading, and I wasn't a reader.

By the time I reached thirty I was embarrassed by my lack of knowledge, and I set out to read the classics. The goal was one a week. I started with *Moby-Dick*. I finished it more than two months later. Alas, I am sure I didn't do Mr. Melville's book justice. James Fenimore Cooper's *The Deerslayer* came next, and the main character, Hawkeye, took my hand and led me into the wilderness of literature. Mark Twain's *A Connecticut Yankee in King Arthur's Court* was the third book I read. After that, I was starved for beautiful words and swallowed whole anything I could find.

More than ten years after being introduced to Chaucer's *Canterbury Tales,* I read them. Twice. His parade of personalities so impressed me that when a girlfriend picked up an abandoned puppy on the side of the road and brought him home and she struggled to come up with a name, I suggested Chaucer.

As late in life as my early thirties, I used to wake up in the middle of the night and wonder when I'd make something of myself. Mostly what I wanted was to be happy and at peace with who I was. But I had no career. Although I always had friends, I rarely fit in, wherever I was. I was still waiting to discover who I'd become.

But looking back on things, every turn in the road, every uphill, every crash contributed to make me who I'd become. When I looked at Atticus and Will and my monastic life, the words of Paulo Coelho in *The Alchemist* came to mind.

"So, I love you because the entire universe conspired to help me find you."

I could have said that to Atticus or Will. But mostly I believe I was saying it to myself. A long path had brought me home, to a world I had always dreamed of, but never knew existed. In spite of all my human frailties, I had come to love myself, and therefore was able to love others. Completely. Selflessly.

Although I was never obsessed with Will's past, I'd sometimes think about how the universe conspired in Will's life to bring him into our home. Readers all know that truth is stranger than fiction. A year and a half into my friendship with Will, I was still perplexed about how he'd found his way into the already set partnership between Atti and me.

But we'd left the past where it belonged and started anew. I urged Will to look at his life as a tabula rasa, a blank slate. Whatever had conspired against him didn't matter to me in the least. What we did with what we had was everything.

It was Martha House who unwittingly revealed an insight into Will's life. One day when we were on the phone she mentioned a painting that hadn't come out the way she wanted it to. She e-mailed me a photo of it, and it was bleak and dark, reminiscent of some back-city alleyway during a power outage.

As we continued to speak, I heard Martha moving around her studio, just as I had been moving around my writing space. Before hanging up, she told me to check my e-mail. While we were talking she had repainted the disappointing canvas, adding zest and light, and two abstract characters in the middle of the scene who looked like they were dancing.

I was moved. She'd changed a piece that wasn't working into one that came alive. It was a redo, just as Will had redone his life. Just as I had changed mine.

Will came to me a mess. He'd been run over by a Mack truck full of crazy, to borrow the line from Marijane. But with care and a second chance, he had made the dark, bleak canvas of his life into something hopeful and sparkling. At the center of Martha's canvas there was dancing. Inside of dear Will, there was also a dancer, and he was emerging.

I could see how far Will had come when I massaged him. He had learned to love, but more important, he had learned to be loved, and he learned to trust. If my fingers came near his mouth when I was gently working my way around his body, he'd open wide, and sometimes he would grab hold, but he'd never bite hard. There were days he'd simply hold them between his teeth, and other times, as when Rachael examined him and he wasn't comfortable, he'd bite slowly at the air.

His instinct was to attack, but he was reminding himself not to.

Will wasn't just aging, he was growing older. I liked that. Even in his elderly years, he was still learning and growing.

Along with the problems with Will's skin, his legs were getting weaker. He was having difficulty standing on the wood floor and on linoleum. Slowly his legs would spread and he'd slide down into a spread-eagle position. He would sink until he lay flat. When he tried to get up again, he couldn't. His front legs would reach out, but he couldn't get traction and he'd slide an inch or two forward each time he fell. This frustrated him to no end, and it also became an issue when he urinated in the house, because he'd slide down into it and not be able to get up.

After watching him struggle like this for several days, I realized that even the bath towels I had been spreading around our apartment weren't working. I had another idea.

I ordered half a dozen yoga mats and covered the bare floors. They were perfect. Will could stand on them and pull himself up while on them, and they were also machine washable.

Life was never easy with Will in it. There was always something to figure out, but that was part of our contract.

His next difficulty was sleeping through the night. His middle-of-the-night rambles around our home were happening so often that I was beginning to suffer from sleep deprivation. Rachael gave him the smallest dose of pill possible to help him sleep. While it worked some nights, on most he'd wake up, and after getting out of bed, he'd start banging into things as if he were a drunk. He'd fall and cry out, whimpering in his confusion.

Since neither one of us liked the effects of the sleeping pills, I stopped giving them to him. My next plan was to attach a small bell to the corner of my bed. Most nights after that, he'd get up and brush against the bell, waking me up. I'd stumble to my feet, hurry to find him, and run him outside, or at least get to him in time to hold him when he went to the bathroom.

When autumn had given way to winter, even as Will was getting weaker, Atticus was having many rough chemotherapy days, and I was wearing down, one afternoon a thought hit me. There, in the middle of our messy lives, with things not at their best, I thought, *I am right where I am supposed to be.*

It was a freeing thought.

I never found my religion in church.

I didn't find it in my angry days playing judge, jury, and executioner in Newburyport.

I found it first in the mountains.

And later I realized it was also in the woods and by the streams and lakes.

When Will arrived and Atticus and I spent more time in the backyard, I found my religion there too, with the blue jays and chipmunks and woodpeckers. And the bears.

Slowly, while we fought cancer, pushed death away, and resisted exhaustion, I understood that religion was also in our home, in these friendships, in the bonds we shared and the most basic of pleasures.

Richard Rohr wrote, "Faith is not for overcoming obstacles; it is for experiencing them—all the way through!"

I discovered the faith I had always longed for in the last place I looked for it—within me.

Life wasn't easy, but it was beautiful. It was filled with grace.

All three of us were indeed right where we were supposed to be.

8

Aragorn and Atticus

Wonder is the heaviest element on the periodic
table. Even a tiny fleck of it stops time.
—DIANE ACKERMAN, *Going on Faith: Writing as a*
Spiritual Quest

When you have Will's past, the challenges come and go.
It's only natural. I understood from the beginning that
nothing was guaranteed. So we took each day as it came, the
good with the bad, the healthy with the sick.

On some of those days, Will slept soundly. He'd be so still
that I'd check to make sure he was breathing. With my hand
on his chest, I could feel it rising up and down, the tiny heartbeat pulsed with my touch. Whenever I did this, he rarely

stirred. In his relaxed state, I'd whisper to him about our original contract. It was a simple one. "I like having you here, and you're welcome to stick around for as long as you wish, but please understand, it's your life to live or leave."

On one of the hottest summer nights, not even the air conditioners seemed to be helping Will. Atticus and I were on the couch in the living room when Will stumbled out of the bedroom. He was dizzy and swaying. I heard the wheezing right away, and when I walked over to him, he pushed himself against me, wanting me to pick him up. I held him and we looked into each other's eyes. It was ironic—those cloudy, old, mostly blind eyes said so much when we came face-to-face and he was in my arms. People talked about how beautiful Will's eyes were, but mostly they were talking about his long black lashes. But his eyes were gorgeous too. They used to be squinty, back when he didn't know who to trust and the pain was difficult to handle. As he gradually shed the pain and confusion, what was left were pools of innocence, deep and sweet.

He rested his chin on my shoulder, and the rattling in his breathing frightened me.

I came close to texting Rachael to ask her to meet us at her office, but I held off for a few minutes. Instead, I took Will outside. The air was as thick as syrup. He coughed and he choked. We returned to get Atticus, I threw a few things in my backpack, and leading by my headlamp, we walked through the ferns and the undergrowth to the river.

I lit tea candles and placed them on the rocks. I turned on music on my phone and plugged it into a small wooden speaker. Vivaldi flowed, just as the Ellis River did down from the mountains, over my ankles, and beyond us on its way to the Atlantic Ocean.

Atticus sat on his flat rock and watched as fireflies flashed and glowed around him and all over the river. They were like stars dancing and swirling among us, daring to be closer to us than to the rest of the firmament high overhead.

Even in the darkness I could see Will's eyes looking into mine. I could hear the wheezing in his chest. The struggle to breathe. The dry rasping. The helplessness.

Nothing is guaranteed, nothing but this moment. I told myself this again and again.

That doesn't just go for elderly dogs and people. It goes for all of us, for all of life. It is forever fleeting. The Appalachian Mountain Club has eight huts located along the Appalachian Trail as it winds across the White Mountains. In one of them hangs an old carved sign: REMEMBER, YOU ARE DYING.

Under a sliver of moon through a gap in the shadowy trees, I carried Will to the middle, where the land rises and the water is shallow. It's the same place he'd sat the day before in the high heat of late morning. I lowered him. He trusted me with his body.

I placed him in the refreshing current and I sat behind him, my legs on either side to give him balance. He lowered the rest of his body. I could hear his tongue lapping at the mountain waters, drinking them in, cooling his throat.

Will's body pushed up against my right leg and he laid his head atop my shin.

Shallow breaths grew deeper. The tension left him. He could inhale again. The rattle disappeared.

There was the flow of the water over the smooth river stones, the hoot of a barn owl, and Vivaldi. Other than that, we were as still as the night.

Upstream, the owl hooted again.

We stayed like that for several minutes, until Will started to shiver. When we stood, I wrapped him a thick towel, draped him over my shoulder, like a happy sack of sand, and went around blowing out the candles. He was comfortable riding this way, his body high, molding to mine, his head hugging my neck.

Atticus led us up the embankment, through the ferns and the fallen trees, over a small tumble of rocks, along the same path Aragorn and the other bears took.

When I looked behind us, there was a parade of fireflies spread out along the route we'd taken from the water. They looked to me like fairy dust trailing in our wake.

We climbed the stairs. Right outside our door, a large spider hovered overhead. I reminded her that she could stay, but to give us space. I did this by blowing softly on her. She retreated to an alcove in the little roof above our deck. This had been our little game for more than a week. After the first few days, her web never seemed to get in our way. All it seemed to take was a gentle reminder for her to respect our space and we'd respect hers.

Inside, I dried Will and sat on the floor with him. My back was against the couch. Atticus laid his head on my shoulder from his regular perch to watch me. I reached over and picked up the water bowl for Will to take another drink. I passed it up to Atticus. By and by we all drifted off. Atticus above us, Will in my arms, and me on the floor.

I woke a couple of hours later, Will still in my arms, Atticus's chin still on my shoulder. There was a wild rumbling outside, brassy and powerful and relentless. A deluge of raindrops on the metal roof. I placed Will in his bed, covered him up, and asked Atticus to make room for me on the couch. He slipped behind my knees as I curled on my side. My one hand hung over the edge and rested on top of Will.

I woke up with the sunrise and the call of the crows. The air was clean, the humidity gone. Crystal skies and green trees glowed before six in the morning. We went outside and Will drank as much of the fresh mountain air as his tired lungs could hold.

The grass was damp and dew shimmered like diamonds.

Back inside, I threw open the windows, turned off the air conditioners, and turned on a fan in my writing room to suck everything through.

Will retreated to the bedroom for a few more hours' sleep. Atticus and I left for the woods. The forest was magnificent— teeming with vitality. We saw a deer gliding ahead of us, and then an enormous spider web across the trail. We walked out of our way to keep it safe.

The early hour and newly scrubbed air made for an easy hike to Table Mountain.

We returned home long before Will woke up. When he did, I moved one of his beds onto the deck and put up a child's gate I picked up so that Will could enjoy the air without tumbling down the stairs if he decided to walk around. I was inside at the kitchen table, processing the photographs from that morning's climb. Through the open door I could feel the gentle draft and hear Will's snores. They were rhythmic and easygoing. He was perfectly relaxed.

It was the kind of mountain morning I imagined before moving north. To get out early on the trails and return home by late morning.

All was well in our little world.

As a drop of condensation ran down my mason jar of iced tea, I saw a movement out on the deck out of the corner of my eye.

Aragorn was close to the top step, with Will right below him and within reach.

He was full grown by now, and his massive paws rested on the top of the gate. His head was close to lying on his paws and he was looming there, watching Will. I didn't move. Slowly, Aragorn turned his head to look at me. I nodded in his direction. He turned back to Will. He studied Will's tiny body as it rose and fell in slumber. It was just the opposite of his first days in Jackson, when he looked broken even in the innocence of sleep. Now he reflected tranquility and belonging.

I took the photo card out of my computer and looked for my camera.

Damn it! It was on the coffee table. I didn't want to break the spell, so I didn't move. Aragorn could have easily ripped through that gate if he wanted, I knew this, but I also knew that was not his intention. I was even surprised that the weight of his paws didn't loosen it.

I could hear the wind chimes and the birdsong. I heard Will's snores, and Aragorn's sniffing.

I wanted a photograph, badly, but when I finally moved to grab my camera, Aragorn left. He padded down the stairs, in no hurry. But he was soon gone.

It wasn't the bear's first close encounter with Will that summer, but it was the *closest*.

The other took place during Bike Week a month before. Every spring the mountains echo with the mechanical roar of motorcycles. I imagine it's fun for the bikers, but it isn't much of a pleasure for those who enjoy quiet. When they are here for a week every year, I often wonder how the wildlife handles the noise, how much it disturbs them. But I think I already know.

There were flowers out on the deck—on the little table,

hanging from the roof frame and along the railing. The door was closed because of the racket. It was early afternoon, and just inside the door, Will slept on the floor. It was one of those days when he fell asleep right where he was. His rump was pressed against the base of the door.

I was at the stove when I saw Aragorn step onto the deck. I hadn't seen him since he'd turned into an adult. A beautiful mammal. Kingly, like the Tolkien character I named him after. He rested his chin on the railing and watched the packs of bikers pass below him in both directions.

He turned his attention to the flowers. Through the glass I took photographs of him smelling them, pawing at the pitcher on the table, as if he was pulling it closer. He didn't bite any of them; he was smelling them, as Will always did.

The bear turned around and looked down on the floor through the glass and saw Will sleeping. He pushed his head closer for a better look. I backed away to see what he would do. Aragorn grabbed Atticus's large dog bed, a hand-me-down from a friend, which I had left on the deck for Atti to use when I was out there writing or reading. To my surprise, Aragorn lay down on the bed, his fanny pushed against the door, opposite Will's.

When he settled down, I took some more photographs of Aragorn taking a nap. The view was resplendent. A little white dog backed up against the door, a full-grown black bear in mirror image on the other side.

Aragorn's serenity wouldn't last forever. The motorcycles were too much, I'm sure, their roar relentless. During one particularly loud thunder of bikes, he jumped, clearly startled, and dashed down the stairs, heading for the woods.

It was an enchanting moment, but that was the last of Atticus's big dog bed outside. I was concerned that Aragorn might have left some ticks behind, so I threw it away and placed another one of Atticus's smaller beds out there for the future.

That was the summer of Aragorn, when we saw him more than any other time. He had a relaxed and stately sway when he moved, and unless he was running, he was stealthy. He was as quiet as a sighing breeze. We'd see him a few times a week, and one morning he was so near I felt his breath on my face.

Will urinated pretty much everywhere. I'm not sure how he did it with the door closed, but it got under the door and the urine sat on the threshold. I had the door open, and was on my hands and knees with cleaning fluid and paper towels. The first I realized Aragorn was close at hand was by his breathing. I looked up. He was only a foot away. The regal black bear was peering at me at eye level.

I'm surprised I didn't have another puddle to clean up.

I didn't move at first. He was so close, I didn't dare. He had never given us reason to fear him before, and I was hoping that was still the case. Ever so cautiously I moved my left leg behind the door and started to ease it closed in slow motion so I didn't startle him. When I felt I could close the door quickly if I needed to, I reached up to the table for my camera and took a few close-ups of Aragorn. It was thrilling and daunting to look into his brown eyes, to see his world there, and to understand that perhaps we weren't very different after all.

As much as I wished we could stay like that, as soon as I was done shooting photos, I said to him, "You know you are not supposed to be up here. If you're not careful, you're going to get yourself in trouble with someone who doesn't like you."

He continued to stare at me, his snout moving. I imagined he was taking in my scent.

I clucked my teeth. "Come on, now, you've got to go!" He half turned, then stopped. He looked back at me. "Off you go."

He retreated down the steps halfway, then the rest, and sat on the grass, just off to the side.

Others in the area knew Aragorn as well. But they didn't see his gentle side. They'd tell me how he growled at them, huffed, and snorted, and snapped his teeth to warn them away. Some were afraid of him. But I never had that feeling. I had no idea what he was thinking, but I never did feel threatened by him, not even when my face was an easy paw-swipe away.

Just as mysterious was one other morning encounter. Atticus and I were sitting on the stone wall that circled the raised gravel patio downstairs. Blue jays were arguing with the crows. The shrieks and the squawks might have been a racket to some, but to me they were preferable to what takes place in the civilized world.

Butterflies were flitting over Will's wildflower garden. Bumblebees darted around the buds of the milkweed plants. A hummingbird buzzed into the yard and fed from the nectar feeder outside our second-floor window.

At that time, we had new neighbors, a man and a woman. They were peaceable enough, I guess, but it's clear they didn't get along with each other. The man skulked around like a frown, and the woman seemed more than happy when he was gone by the way I'd hear her whistling when he had left for work and she was working in the garden. I didn't dislike her or him, I just kept to myself. I'd wave to them and say good morning. She'd say hello, he'd grumble.

There was one thing I didn't like about her, though. It was the way she was pleased that their dog, a large black fellow of indeterminate heritage, chose to pass through the bushes to go the bathroom in our yard. I wouldn't have minded if it wasn't for fear of Will stepping in the large piles or falling in them, and the fact that twice, when he came running into our yard, a cyclone of fur and enthusiasm, he came close to knocking Will over.

Will was sleeping inside that day.

In that lazy drifting way a summer day starts with sunlight slanting in from the side, bugs of all sizes were caught in the rays and looked like fairies. It would grow hot a little later, and the cool morning air was reason to loiter. We were just as carefree as the winged souls we were watching.

Atticus leaned into me. I returned the favor. But the further he leaned, the less typical it felt. He looked up at me and then to his left. I followed his look. Fifteen feet away, just behind us, Aragorn moseyed into the yard. He looked over at us casually. I wasn't sure how I felt about his being just behind us, so I turned to face him.

That's when he sat down. And like the two of us, he seemed delighted to relax and watch the activity in our yard. The birds, the bugs, the bees visiting Will's wildflower garden were a study in busyness. Occasionally Aragorn turned to look at us, but always returned his gaze to the garden. When the crows flew to the top of the black ash tree, he turned his head to watch them.

Five, ten, fifteen minutes he sat there, as blissful, it seemed, as we were, as still as Atticus used to sit on a mountain. He moved only his head and his eyes.

I had my camera with me hoping to capture photos of butterflies. It was my lucky day; instead I took a couple of hundred photos of Aragorn. I captured the way he sat and turned his head to look at us. It turned out I didn't need that many shots of him, because he barely moved from photo to photo. That's how composed he was.

He was silent and serene until I finally heard him give off a loud *huff,* then a few snaps of his jaws. That's when the woman next door came out of her house. He couldn't see her, because the brush was too thick and high, but he obviously heard her, or maybe it was her scent. He grew louder and more agitated. More huffing, more snapping, always looking toward the neighbor's yard. His anxiety rose. He rocked back and forth, and then he exploded from his sitting position and ran right into the neighbors' yard, first at her, and then back toward the river.

She complained to me about how he kept getting into her trash, including the night before, and talked of calling the animal control officer. I suggested that if she did, I'd have to do the same about her shitting dog.

"Maybe it would be wiser to put your trash where the bears can't get at it. It would be better for you and for them in the long run."

That couple didn't last very long next door, and we were left without human neighbors for a long while after that. I didn't mind a bit.

There are many things in life I'll never understand, among them Aragorn's regular visits. My romantic heart would love to imagine it had something to do with Will and his growing innocence. But the truth is, Atticus was the true magnet for wild animals. He'd sit still when around them, and they'd prepare to dash off, but when he never growled or barked or gave chase, they relaxed as well.

Still, no matter what brought the bears to our yard, when Will was around they were kinder to him and more curious. They'd be mesmerized by his dance and look at him interestedly as they passed through, and sometimes I'd see a bear in the brush on the edge of our property, watching him. They'd stop what they were doing to take in his circling dance.

An expert on bears might have an opinion, but I'm not sure I'd care to hear it. I prefer that bit of the unknown—that sliver left for possibilities we may not understand, things that we may leave to our instincts.

For example, as I've written, Atticus avoided Will, except on the rarest of occasions. I am convinced that Atti would have been very happy if Will had never come to live with us, and would be happy when he was gone. Still, there is a tenderness to Atticus that I admire, even if much of it remains inexplicable.

I recall a morning at the White Mountain Café, one of the incarnations of the bakery next to Carrie's flower shop that has changed hands several times in the last six years. Atticus and I went inside so I could order an iced coffee. He sat by the swinging gate leading behind the counter and waited while they brought his bowl of water to him. It was a morning routine. A family of four sat at a nearby table. The girls, about three and five years old, were watching Atticus, and I told their parents that he was good with children and not to worry.

The smaller girl got down on the floor with him.

"Do you mind if she pets you, Atticus?"

He kept his eyes on me while she stroked his hair. She moved closer to his face and looked at him. Her older sister watched from the table, as did the parents. I asked the girl at the table if she wanted to pat Atticus. She shook her head no, but continued to watch her sister.

We saw them the next morning too. Again, after Atticus got his bowl of water, the smaller girl got down on the floor with him. A minute later, her sister joined her and started petting Atticus. It was so natural I didn't think anything of it.

Atticus turned all his attention to the older sister. He took to her as if they'd known each other before. She'd pet him, then stop, and smile and giggle as he used his nose on her hand to ask for another caress.

I noticed a queer look on their mother's face as I chatted with the father.

When we left, I wished the family well on the rest of their vacation. But the mother followed us outside.

"Can I talk to you, please?"

"Sure, what's up?"

"It's Atticus . . . your dog."

"What about him?"

Her eyes started to water and she couldn't speak. She turned to compose herself and put her hand to her mouth. She took some deep breaths.

"My daughter . . . my older daughter . . ." More tears.

She wiped her sleeve across her nose.

"Sorry, but my older daughter's never done that before."

"What do you mean?'

"We have no idea what happened to her, but she has an irrational fear of dogs. My husband, he had her on his shoulders at a Memorial Day parade back home, and when a dog went by she started screaming. It wasn't the first time. It's always happened. She's terrified of dogs."

She blew her nose on the napkin I gave her. "We have been at wit's end about it. It's so bad we have her seeing a psychologist. He can't explain it either. There's no rational reason for why she gets paralyzed."

I suggested maybe it was because Atticus was smaller.

"That's not it. Size doesn't matter. She screams as if she's going out of her mind even with the smallest dogs. When you came in with Atticus yesterday, I was surprised she was okay. But to see her on the floor with him, I . . . I . . . I just don't know. He's different, isn't he?"

"I think he is," I said, smiling, "but I've never asked him about it."

Before we left she threw her arms around my neck and hugged me.

"Thank you. You don't know how much it means."

Her husband and her daughters came out then, and the husband came over and shook my hand. "Thank you," he said. "You have no idea."

On a night when Will's seizures wouldn't stop, coming one after another until he lay in a state of exhaustion, I picked him up and put him on the bed with us. I waited for Atticus to hop down and leave the room; he never liked Will on the furniture and departed as soon I'd pick up Will. Instead he moved closer and laid his head against Will's. One of his floppy ears covered Will's face at first. Will had been breathing the way people do when they sob. With Atticus pushing up against him, their heads looking like yin and yang with both lying in opposite directions, Will quickly recovered his composure. We all stayed on the bed until Will wanted to get down.

It was only the third time Atticus had ever approached Will.

The next night, when I brought Will up on the bed with Atticus and me, sure enough, Atticus jumped to the floor and went into the other room. I found him on the couch.

I think the Universe was telling me it's a good thing I stopped looking for definites in a world of mystery. For it's not like I could explain much of this anyway. It really did feel like a fairy tale. The interaction of Atticus with Will, being there for him only when he needed it most, just as Marijane predicted. The way Aragorn and the other bears moved gently around Will. More important, how all animals seemed to find peace when near Atticus.

Atticus often calmed wild animals, sitting with them only yards away. There was Amelia, the wayward woodpecker who used to fly to the suet feeder hanging on our back door. When the door was open, she'd have her fill at the feeder and then fly right inside the house. I'd catch her with a small trash can with some cardboard over the top, but after a few times I didn't need the cardboard, and eventually she just let me use my hands.

But here's the thing—I always had a sense she was flying inside to get a better look at Atticus. She would land on the feeder with him on a stool right in front of it. No other bird did that. She would let Atticus press his nose against her body without flying off.

During our first summer living in Jackson, a female chipmunk used to flirt with Atticus. He'd be outside and she'd pop up somewhere and squeak at him. He'd race to her, but not before she disappeared. A few seconds later she'd show up in the high grass or the stone wall. He'd run to her again, and she'd disappear. One afternoon she climbed a birch sapling right outside our door. It was only five feet tall. She grasped it and watched Atticus looking at her. She didn't squeak or act frightened and their eyes met. When he sat, she watched him without moving. Her flirtation didn't work. He didn't move until we went back inside to the writing room. I left the door open. He was napping beside my desk. Movement caught my eye. I looked up and saw it was the chipmunk. She had crept to the doorway and was peering around the edge to look at Atticus sleeping. She looked at me. I gave her a shrug. She moved closer to him. Closer. Closer yet. He raised an eyelid. She paused. He opened both eyes and looked at her a foot away. It reminded me of that scene from *The Hobbit* when Bilbo goes into the Lonely Mountain and comes face-to-face with Smaug, the dragon. But Atticus wasn't biting. He wasn't growling. He was merely being Atticus.

He went back to sleep. I was probably too boring for her, because when he decided to nap, she didn't stick around for me. She stole stealthily across the kitchen and out the back door.

One morning, Atticus and I decided to climb South Doublehead. It was early. When we left Will sleeping at home, the crows cawed at us as we descended the stairs. Just over an hour later, we were sitting on the south ledges near the summit, sharing a pack of peanut butter crackers. We both heard a squawk and looked in the direction of the noise. Where

A winter moment on the beach in Provincetown, Massachusetts.

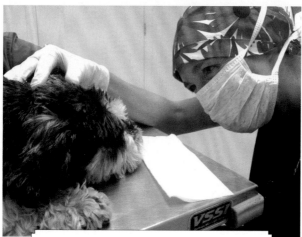

Dr. Rachael Kleidon consults with Atticus.

Aragorn, here barely fifteen feet away, spending time in the backyard with us, watching the comings and goings of butterflies, bees, and hummingbirds.

Rachael with our thank you gifts to the
staff at North Country Animal Hospital.

TOP LEFT: "I must have flowers, always, and always." —Claude Monet. TOP RIGHT: The Will Wagon. BOTTOM LEFT: "I'm so glad I live in a world where there are Octobers." —L.M. Montgomery. BOTTOM RIGHT: Will and Ann Stampfer sharing some wisdom . . . or maybe comparing their hairstyles.

During the warmer months Will often soaked in the lyric water running down from the mountains on its way to the ocean.

The loveliest of goodbyes.

Will doing Atticus things, sitting in Iron Mountain meadow in front of Agiocochook and several of the higher peaks of his enchanted forest.

the pine trees stopped, a large crow was sitting on a branch watching us.

I put some cracker down on my left, while Atticus sat on my right. It didn't take long for that crow to join us for a mountaintop snack. I'd give some to Atti, break off some for the crow, then take a nibble myself. We sat with that crow for twenty minutes. The bird wasn't the least bit bothered by sharing crackers and a view with two mammals.

On another day, down the road from our home, a line of cars had pulled over at a pond. I slowed down. A moose was eating some vegetation. There were probably a hundred people watching that moose do her thing.

Moose are mind-boggling, the way they move like machines with those stilt legs. It seems almost unnatural. But when they run, they can move quickly, reaching speeds up to thirty-five miles an hour. You don't want to encounter one during rutting season when you are out in the woods.

While the crowd watched the moose, Atticus and I circled around to sit by ourselves. Moose don't have the best vision, but their sense of smell is keen. She looked up at me and Atticus, then down again, then back up at us, eating calmly all the while. A large man with an even larger mouth on the other side of the pond started yelling at me to get Atticus out of there.

"She'll charge that dog, you idiot!"

At first I ignored him. But it was increasingly difficult to do, the more he yelled at us.

"She's going to charge. Get out of there!"

Atticus was calm. So was the moose. I'd seen him this way around moose before. It's the way he was with all animals. The shared calm was surreal, but it was also what I'd come to expect from him.

The man kept yelling and yelling. He was red in the face. Eventually, he was right—the moose charged! But it didn't charge us, it charged him, and he had to move quickly out of the way.

I once came upon something Emerson wrote about Thoreau after he died: "His intimacy with animals suggested what Thomas Fuller records of Butler the apiologist, that 'either he had told the bees things or the bees had told him.'"

It's hard to understand how souls communicate. I can tell you perhaps a hundred or a thousand reasons why I love someone. But none of that explains love, and how it happens. Why do people who are similar fall in love? How do opposites reach the same plane? Then there are those from different species who find a bond. Miracles are indeed everywhere.

Will's resiliency gave me daily lessons in groundedness, while Atticus taught the mysteries of the spirit.

Perhaps his biggest lesson for me is not to underestimate a soul, no matter the size of the body, no matter the breed, species, race, or religion. The unexplained offers us reasons to exercise our faith. Maybe that's why Atticus was in my life, to show me not to limit life's possibilities. Anything can happen.

And there it is again, the idea of Atticus and infinitude.

9

Grace

It is not down on any map; true places never
are.

—HERMAN MELVILLE

There were days when I looked around and thought, *How
did things get so good when I used to be so bad?*

Will's second winter arrived, and one morning it found
me holding a mug of peppermint tea. Snow fell heavily onto
the edge of enchantment. It filled up the backyard, and with
the help of the wind, it left behind smooth drifts. The stubble of Will's wildflower garden broke through the swells, and
the old black ash tree was made to look young again with a
layer of frosting over every branch and twig. Cardinals and

chickadees would alight on the bird feeders, taking their share of sunflower seeds while the woodpeckers drilled at the suet feeders. I scattered bread crumbs for the crows to eat. They'd call out to me until I arrived, and after I spread their feast before them they became quiet, reverential, and waited until I walked away before swooping down for a landing.

Atticus was stretched out on the couch, his head atop a cushion, his cancer and chemotherapy an afterthought. It was another mountain we'd climbed together, and on the other side of it he was all he'd ever been, save for a missing toe.

Will was curled in his bed under the tree, diving deep into slumber while Sinéad O'Connor seduced him with her version of "Silent Night." He was wrapped in his handmade quilts, looking like the rest of the presents scattered about him. Above him, the tiny white Christmas lights pierced the gloom like the first stars at dusk, and shiny ornaments reflected their hope.

I took it all in. The soft snores, the flicker of flames on each of the lit candles swaying to a draft I couldn't feel, the cinnamon sticks simmering in a pot atop the stove, their aroma adding to the coziness.

How is it possible, I asked myself, that I'd arrived at a place in life where everything felt perfect? A man like me, who had made so many bad choices and mistakes, was waylaid by detours and false hopes, and wasn't always smart enough to get out of the way of the Mack trucks full of crazy?

The snow had turned everything into a wonderland, but I knew it would one day melt. I knew that Will might not make it to another Christmas, and that, yes, Atticus was getting older as well, and would eventually leave me behind. Yet I felt blessed.

It wasn't that my life was actually perfect. But in that peaceful quiet, tucked away from the hurry and angst of the rest of the world, we were all in a special place. A place we'd made together. Marijane used to tell me, "You've been given the gift of grace."

It was not the best winter for Will. Storm after storm battered the mountains, and our driveway was the only place he could trundle around and dance. We'd have to wait for the plow to come, and for me to shovel a pathway, because the deep snow out back would have swallowed him whole. The red coat I'd bought for him a few months ago was essential. He'd changed so much since the previous winter, when he was able to go without a coat. He was no longer as robust. He'd lost weight, and much of his sensitive skin was shaved to allow access to medicated ointments. Will didn't mind the loss of hair; it relieved him to have his itch tended to. Before I had shaved his front legs, he'd stretch them out in front of him and chew them bloody. The treatment never cured his skin, but it did make it less sensitive. Rachael Kleidon thought his continued skin problems were a sign that Will was winding down, although tests didn't show anything more.

I thought of Will as one of the many Subarus I'd seen around the mountains. "A good winter car," people would say. Others referred to it as the state car of New Hampshire. But a mechanic once warned me against getting one. "Good engine," he said, "but the body rusts out first."

Was Will a Subaru? With his body already broken in so many ways, and now skin that would never completely heal.

Thank goodness for Rachael. Will had not had a cross moment since the day he sat in my arms atop Pine Mountain the previous year. He had become an exemplary patient whenever we went to see her. He'd relax as she scooped him up and held him in a sitting position and gently bounced him in her arms.

The Metacam, regular stretching, and nourishing food helped take away his old pains. On one office visit I cradled Will on his back. When Rachael came in the room, I showed her our new trick. Gently I tossed him in the air a few inches and caught him. His eyes grew bright and airy. Again I tossed him, this time higher, and he landed back in my arms. On the third toss I caught him and brought him up to my face, where he licked me and wanted to play.

Although she'd seen him regularly since becoming his vet, she couldn't fathom how the dog she met the first time a year and a half before was improving that much while he approached his seventeenth birthday.

"I think he found the Fountain of Youth!" she said. "I cannot believe how far he's come, and how sweet he is."

Before we said good-bye to Rachael, I put his red coat on him and pulled the belt tight to make up for his weight loss.

"Maybe it's not the Fountain of Youth," Rachael joked. "Maybe it's his coat. It's like Superman's cape!"

Yes, angry Will had risen from his ruin and had become quite sweet, with puppy-like innocence in a limited body. He liked playing, and even turned out to be mischievous. He'd often try to catch me in the house, with his front paws lunging for my ankles. To please him, I'd sometimes pretend to fall down when he did this, and he'd half trot to me in his slow-motion gait. When he reached me I'd pick him up and roll him onto his back on my chest, where I'd pretend to wrestle with him.

It was remarkable, really.

He was slowing down, having a more difficult time standing and keeping his balance, but he was healthier from the inside out.

His fans couldn't get enough of Will. They'd sigh and cry while watching the Willabies, and cheer him when he gave chase to me in videos. When I'd put a vase of fresh blooms in front of him, a gift from one of his many new friends, he'd inhale, then sit looking up at me while I took a photograph of him behind the arrangement.

When Will came to live with us, there were six thousand people following Atticus and me on Facebook. A year later it had risen to twelve thousand. When Atticus started his battle with cancer two months after that, the numbers jumped up by an additional fifty thousand by the early fall. By midwinter, there were more than a hundred thousand people checking in to see how Will and Atticus were doing.

From time to time I'd think about those numbers, and it had me considering the choices I made in moving north toward simplicity with Atticus. I didn't have much money. Didn't own a house or drive a nice car, but on a daily basis, as I wrote about simplicity and Atti's sense of self and Will's redemption, I was fortified that I'd made the right decisions. It wasn't so much the number of people who were logging in each day, it was what they had to say. In their words I could see that they too longed for such things. The very idea of standing still on top of a mountain, of watching bears come and go, of being covered by a blanket, or of having a pie baking in the oven brought out the best in folks. It touched on something that had more to do with being than owning something, of feeling complete and feeling nurtured, or of having a simpler life.

I think that by watching Will and Atticus, people connected with their own needs and desires.

As February rushed along, Will made the most of his time outside in the small square of driveway that wasn't covered by snow. He'd chase after me in a circle, or dance, even lifting off one day in such an astonishing way that he balanced on his rear lags as he stood. He'd dropped down—bounce, bounce, bounce—and then spring up again. With each succeeding attempted jump, he stood taller and happier. It was a jubilant dance, and it mimicked the tantrums he used to throw when I carried him into the apartment and placed him on the floor.

In the snow, with his red coat with its white collar, he looked like he belonged with jolly old Saint Nick.

Back inside, he fell asleep before I could even get his coat off him.

He was cheerier, but he now lacked the endurance he had built up before.

One afternoon, a package arrived from Anne Criscitiello, a Facebook follower. It was large and flat and tightly secured with layers of tape. I took out a knife and sliced at the seams. When I opened it, a note fell out first.

Anne had been battling cancer for years, and while she'd always been an artist, she had forsaken art and did all she could to survive by holding on to herself. She had lost the inspiration to draw and paint. But after reading *Following Atticus* and becoming fans of Atti and Will on Facebook, she wrote that for the first time in five years she had drawn something. When I cut through the last of the packaging, I beheld a spectacular sketch of Will, Atticus, and me. She'd had it framed and matted. I was taken aback when I read Anne's letter, knowing what our story had done for her, and seeing the results in that remarkable drawing.

I e-mailed Marijane and sent a photo of the drawing. She wrote back: "Good things are happening, Tommy. People are changing because of Atticus and Will—and don't forget that you have something to do with that too. You three make a great team! The drawing is perfect. My paintings and drawings never turn out like Anne's. To think this is her first try in five years. That humbles me."

Anne, I would learn, preferred being called Annie. I had read about her struggles with cancer through her comments on our Facebook page. I had a mutual friend get her phone number for me, and on a Sunday, I surprised her with a call. From the first time we talked, we were friends. She told me about how badly she wanted to move from Brooklyn to a little farm in Vermont one day, and spend her life with goats. She longed for simplicity. We discussed her dance with cancer, and I was lifted by her spirit. She was sweet but tough, an impassioned fighter who was determined to live no matter how often the cancer came back. We talked of Atticus and his own cancer treatments, and of course we talked of Will. Will was continuing to grow into himself, and as his heart expanded, so did the ripples of his story.

He inspired Annie and thousands of others with his decision to reclaim what he had lost.

He'd been an afterthought—discarded in a shelter when he was fifteen, bound to be euthanized—until fate stepped in. Will's story transfixed people.

I'd started the Facebook page at the request of my publisher's marketing department, as a way to talk about our story and communicate about events. But I never expected so many people to invest in us, or that I would become so invested in them as they shared their stories—in quick glimpses or in lengthy, moving comments. Annie represented many who had cancer. There were others with kidney disease or heart issues, and still others who'd lost someone dear to them. As people reached out on the page and many others responded to them, minds and hearts were opened. New friends made themselves vulnerable by writing about what has hurt them, or a dream lost or undertaken. People wrote of their greatest joys, their darkest fears. Friendships formed away from our page, online communities sprang up, and people took trips to visit one another, whether across the state, the country, or the ocean. Those who started out following Atticus were now following Atticus, rooting on Will, and supporting each other in ways large and small.

I'd smile as I read these stories and saw how familiarity blossomed among strangers who became acquaintances and then dear friends.

Will received a new handmade blanket at least every other week, sometimes via a package to our friend Laura Cummings at White Birch Books. Whenever a parcel came in for Will, I'd sit on the floor with him and open it up. He'd bounce in anticipation because he knew whenever I did that, I had something for him.

We knew that the clouds of cataracts meant he couldn't see very much, but it was almost always enough. He would always have difficulty seeing smaller treats, and he'd often overlook them even if they were right in front of him. But he never missed a flower, whether a lone wildflower in the yard or the bouquets he often received. Whenever I'd come home with flowers for him, or Carrie would deliver a vase, he'd know immediately. If he could have, he would have jumped up to greet them. Instead he'd take the smallest, quickest leaps with his front paws. Up and down, up and down in excitement.

Aunt Marijane loved hearing about the latest bag of treats that was sent for Will and Atticus. I read her the more poignant notes and sent pictures of each new bouquet Will received. When I told her Will had received more than twenty-five quilts, prayer shawls, and crocheted afghans made especially for him by women who would never meet him, she spoke about the miracle of kindness.

Marijane was in her late seventies and still quite active. Her mind was sharp, although seemingly once a week I'd have to talk her through a computer issue. It was one of the rare times I'd hear her grumble. She had a good, healthy ego, and would inform me that there had to be something wrong with her laptop because "I'm not dumb. I know what I'm doing." I'd laugh at her lie, and so would she when she realized I was onto her.

"Perhaps I should send you things via carrier pigeon. I know it's outdated, but technology seems to be a challenge for you."

"It's not me, it's technology. They change it every week."

"Oh, I just remembered—a while ago you said you wrote me a Christmas card, but it never came. I thought I'd let you know."

"I did write a Christmas card to you, and Atticus and Will. But I haven't sent it yet. I should do that."

"Yes, I'd love to see it, especially since it is March."

"Don't fear. You'll have it by Easter."

The only other time I heard her be less than charitable was when she railed against the conservative social positions of the Republicans who controlled the Arizona government. For the most part she wasn't much different from the young nun who went west in her early thirties, bringing along her guitar, songs, laughter, and desire to help people. She was still spending several hours a day helping others, but there were days I'd hear the effort in her voice. Always the nurse, therapist, and loyal friend, she'd let me know how this friend was doing or how that person was getting along after a stroke.

I could hear that good soul of hers pulsating across the country, and I understood why the Navajos said she "walked in beauty." She held a reverence for every person she helped, a kindness and compassion. She'd been put in this world to help, and she radiated love and empathy as she did it.

Marijane was everything I'd ever wished for in family but had never found until we became close. My parents, Isabel and Jack, would come to life when she'd tell me stories about their younger years, and I'd get to know them all over again. She'd talk about my mother's MS, and my father's moodiness when he was a teenager.

"She saved him, you know. Your mother saved your father. He always meant well, but he struggled with his moods. He chose to see what was wrong with the world, and would even imagine there was a plot against him. I'd let him have his beliefs. He wasn't going to change. It's one of those things you overlook when you love somebody.

"In those years when you and he were not talking, he never said a bad word about you. He'd always say, 'Out of all my children, Tom's the most like me.'"

"Really? Do you think I am?"

"In a lot of ways. In the ways that I loved about him. You

do things for me that he used to do. I'll talk about a book I want to read, and you'll send it to me. I'll get a card from you, and there will be a check in it, just because. That's the part of you that's like Jack. He could be so kind.

"He would have been so proud of all of this. You being a published author would have given him something to brag about, even if he wouldn't have said a word to you about it. He'd tell me. He always did."

When Marijane and I talked, there were few limitations. She'd even ask me about my sex life.

"I'm not going there, Marijane."

"Why? We talk about everything else. It's part of your life."

"I don't mind telling you about my relationships, but I feel a little uncomfortable discussing my sexual history."

"Fine, I'm here if you want to talk about it."

"And why would I do that?"

"Because I'm a good listener. You know I am."

"And you're also a seventy-eight-year-old virgin."

"Oh, you'd be surprised!"

"What? You're not a virgin? How many lovers have you been with?"

"Um . . . none, but I've counseled many. You would be surprised what I know."

"I'd rather not know."

We'd go on in this way, the laughter building the longer the conversation went, until finally we laughed so hard our bellies hurt. Before hanging up, she'd add, "Remember, if you need to talk about that part of your life, I'm here."

"And I'm hanging up now. I love you."

"I love you too. Walk in beauty."

Marijane never failed to ask about her friend Atticus, and about Will, whom she'd never met. We talked about us taking a road trip out to see her, but I wasn't sure about bringing Will that great a distance. I'd already decided against a return trip to Provincetown in February, because I didn't feel he was up to it. Mostly what he needed was just what he was getting: quiet time, care, good food, flowers, music, and friendship.

Will would still dance and give a half spin in a drunken fit of love for me, but his endurance was waning. As the weeks passed, his skin became even more sensitive, and I took to bathing him once a day. He enjoyed my attention, even if he couldn't stand up on the bath mat in the tub as he had in previous months. He was patient when I lathered him up and rinsed him off.

Sometimes Atticus would come in to watch us as I bathed Will. Together like this, seventeen-year-old Will seemed younger than Atticus, who was twelve, between Atti's stoic nature and Will's reclaimed sense of wonder.

One evening, while Atticus was on the couch and Will was sleeping, I went to shave. I looked at my reflection as I smoothed the cream over my chin and cheeks. There were lines under my eyes, the result of addressing Will's nighttime needs. But even with those lines, I noticed something in my eyes that hadn't been there a few years ago. I saw an ocean of calm. My body was tired, but my spirit had grown peaceful.

Life has a strange way of leading you to where you need to

be. Atticus and I were barely hiking any longer, and I believe we both missed it. My bank account was depressingly low. Will needed attention nearly twenty-four hours a day, and I wondered how long I could go on like that. But I saw in my reflection the same calm and warmth I had always heard in Marijane's voice.

I felt a soft poke against my lower leg. It was Will, looking up at me with eyes earnest and bright. They had never been so big or so kind. I dropped down to my hands and knees to face him. I kissed him and he rubbed his head against mine. When I stood up again, he stayed to watch me finish shaving. He leaned against the door, seeming like a friend I'd known for years.

Will and Atticus were continuing to motivate people like Annie, helping them to believe again when life may have been cruel or callous. My two friends were like kites in the wind, and as they floated by, people saw them and were lifted as well.

I'd read testimonials from people who'd been in the hospital for weeks recovering from a stroke or an amputation or some other serious operation and were inspired by Will to not only live, but live well. Widows wrote to say they'd been heartbroken and in despair but used the example of Will to help them go on. And a particular kind of story was especially moving to me, hearing from people who'd lost a dog or cat and feared loving and losing another. Many people wrote to say they were opening their hearts again—and choosing this time to adopt an elderly animal they'd never have given a second glance to in the past.

Will and Atticus were changing their corner of the world, lifting up those who witnessed their lives on our Facebook page.

When I turned back to the mirror to wash off the rest of the shaving cream, I looked into my own eyes again. I'd never really done that before. Perhaps I was afraid of what I'd see, or maybe it was what I wouldn't. But on that frigid winter night, while the snow was falling yet again and winds lashed at the house and the door rattled and windows shook, I understood that I too had been changed. I had something more than contentment—perhaps I was full of what matters, and no longer fearful of what didn't.

A week later, while I was on the phone with Marijane, she told me her shoulder was hurting after a fall. It wasn't healing the way she expected it to. There were other aches and pains, things she didn't complain about typically. It got worse, and a home health aide came to help her until she felt well enough to take care of herself again.

By the time spring arrived, Marijane was in the hospital. The saintly woman who had so often ministered hospice care was suddenly receiving it herself. We talked a few times on the phone. I could hear she was tired and weak, but she was in good spirits. I told her I would call her again.

The phone rang the next day. It was Marijane's closest friend, Julie. Doctors didn't think she'd make it through the night, and she wanted to say good-bye. Her voice was strained, but even then the calmness was there. I could feel it as we spoke our last words to each other. She promised to say hello to my father for me.

I said, "How do you know you'll see him up there? He could be *down* there."

Even at the end of our days, there was laughter. A few more

words were spoken, I told her I loved her and she said the same to me. Then the words were harder to come by on both ends.

There was a shattering pause. I listened for anything.

I waited.

"Tommy . . ." Marijane was very quiet now. Her words were slow. "Tell Atticus I love him. Walk in beauty, you two."

Walk in beauty.

Those were the last words she said to me. She died peacefully the following night.

For much of the rest of the day I sat thinking about her.

I didn't sob breathlessly or mourn until I got sick. I sat still, as she used to do for hours on days she meditated. I took breaks for Will or to get some water. Other than that, it was stillness. Marijane was not frightened at the end. She accepted it.

I looked at the pile of books we'd read together. Thumbed through some of them, put them back on the table. One at a time I picked them up and flipped through the pages. They were dog-eared, highlighted, underlined, and scribbled in. In the margins I'd find words I'd scratched and others Marijane had brought up that I wrote in my copy. The books, the notes, the lived-in pages—they were like old maps shared by nephew and aunt. They'd taken us this far together. Now we were apart. But I didn't feel lost. And I didn't feel I needed the maps anymore.

Instead, I closed my eyes and thought of her—and there she was. Not far away. I could hear the laughter and her wisdom, the way she listened.

She would have smiled to know that when I opened my eyes, Atticus was sitting on the couch, just a few inches away, staring at me. We were off to walk the trails to the forest and to heed their invitation to "come closer, come closer."

That night, when I tucked Will in to an old Andrews Sisters recording of "Don't Sit Under the Apple Tree (with Anyone Else but Me)," I watched him drift, feeling safe under a quilt.

I played the song repeatedly.

Two and a half years before, when Marijane was on the book tour with Atticus and me, I surprised her by pulling the song up on my phone and plugged it into the car speakers. That night, on a long ride back from Northshire Books in Vermont, I could see the tears flowing down my aunt's face. She grabbed at my hand and held it tight. She continued to look away from me out the passenger-side window.

It was the only time I heard her cry.

We held hands until the song finished.

"You remembered. You remembered when I told you that Jack used to sing this to me when he came back from the war and I was so young."

10

Celery

Animals share with us the privilege of having a soul.
—PYTHAGORAS

The word that most often came to mind while playing with Will in our backyard was *numinous*. There was something charmed and spiritual in his transformation. In the hours of soft light, early in the day, and late, when shade stretched out on the grass, he often seemed to glow. If a shaft of light was slanting down, it always appeared to catch him and follow him as he circled and trotted.

His had become a full life, with every little flower and weed the object of several minutes of devotion. In the lazy summer days, he luxuriated in the cooler hours, then found refuge under the flow of the air conditioners when the sun was overhead. He'd sleep that part of the day away. When the air conditioners were off, he'd pant, so they were on most of the time from May through the remaining summer months. But he still wanted his quilts piled up on top of him when he slept.

When the sun dropped behind the tall trees out back, we'd return to the yard, with the crows and chipmunks never too far away and always watching him, clucking and chattering. They'd be out of sight, but as soon as we came down the stairs, the crows would come flying and land on branches just above us.

While they watched him, Will kept his eye on me, making sure I was never far from him. His wildflower garden thrived, filled with color and butterflies. Bees zipped this way and that to collect their pollen. The pumpkin patch looked hopeful. The whole yard, which would never be seen in a *Better Homes & Gardens* spread, was our own timeless Garden of Eden, where anything seemed possible. Guided in part by Will, I was allowed glimpses into a world I might not have noticed before.

Many a morning I'd lie next to Will, both of us on our bellies, looking at miniature strawberries hidden in the grass, or the bright yellow of a dandelion, or an unknown purple flower. He'd sniff everything. I would too, because I wanted to see what Will's world was like, and appreciate his way of appreciating it.

On those afternoons, with Atticus sitting in one of the Adirondack chairs while I was on the other, Atti enjoyed playing the sentinel. I followed his eyes to see the slightest movements around us. Never chasing, but always capturing the lives of nature scurrying, flying, and hopping about.

Atticus was showing no ill effects from his chemotherapy. His missing toe was never an issue. We still got out for hikes, but they were shorter because Will needed me at home more. Gone were the marathon treks of the past. Rarely did we go more than six miles, but I didn't miss it all that much. I was still finding what I needed. And I think Atticus was too. He always enjoyed our times away on the trails when it was just the two of us, or on the rare occasion when we joined Ken and Ann.

I could always tell when Atticus needed a hike. It was about the same time I did. We'd both get restless. He'd sit by my backpack or at the back door. When we'd go outside, if we hadn't hiked lately, he'd sit by the car. He had his ways of making himself heard.

We concentrated on less known mountains, which were still profound in their ways. We were introduced to many of these by Ken and Ann, who had been hiking for more than forty years, although we returned the favor by taking them to Pine Mountain and Thorne Pond.

Less strenuous didn't mean less exceptional. A mountain doesn't know how big or small it is. It simply is. It doesn't get caught up in the mundane the way we do while massaging our egos, or being urged onward to always do more, to always keep up with others. Increasingly, I understood that happiness comes at the places where we can be still.

Finding the right match of activity and stillness had become my quest. Whenever we set out to hike, I'd choose three trails relatively close to each other. If the first parking lot was crowded, we'd go to the next. If that was just as busy, we'd go to a third. It was easy enough to find a mountain that was not popular on a particular day or a given time. We'd often set out before sunrise and arrive at home by ten in the morning, already having had a full day. At other times, we'd wait until sunset, when everyone else would have finished hiking, or nearly so.

In that quiet, in the calm we'd find on a hidden ledge or on a summit without others around, without cell-phone conversations or selfie addicts clicking away to fill up their Instagram feed, we found what we needed.

Back in our home, I had to be on call for Will, but on a mountain path, we replenished our peace and our need for exploration. It was in the stillness that we fed our souls, but in movement where we spread our wings.

New Hampshire's landscape was still teaching me what I needed to know. The forest had been my classroom and my church; it educated me and centered me. But my continuing education didn't stop there.

I had long ago set out to teach Atticus to be gentle in considering all life, but after those years with him, and our time with Will, and the comings and goings throughout our little patch of land *halfway to wild* of those who were not domesticated, I realized that it was my time to learn more about what being *gentle* meant. Richard Bach was correct in *Illusions* when he wrote, "We teach best what we most need to learn."

For half a century, I never gave much thought to what I ate. Big Macs, Whoppers, buckets of Kentucky Fried Chicken, Wendy's, Pizza Hut, and Ben & Jerry's were all washed down with two liters of Coke or Pepsi a day. My vegetable of choice was french fries, or whatever was layered on my burgers and subs. But that started to change when I began spending time with Susan Carter. She was the daughter of a friend, and she had been a vegetarian since before she was ten years old. Susan was an excellent cook, and if we had plans to have dinner at her house, she'd ask what I wanted.

"I'll just have whatever you're making."

"I'm a vegetarian, but I don't mind cooking meat for others. I do it all the time."

"Thanks, but I'll have what you're having."

"Really?"

"Sure."

During my meals with Susan, I began to discover foods like quinoa and kale. I'd never heard of them before. The meals I had been eating before Susan introduced me to whole foods were made from ingredients that came from a science lab. For the first time in my life, I started appreciating broccoli and asparagus, things that used to make me gag when I was younger. Not that we had them very often when I was growing up. Supper was always pork chops, fried chicken, or London broil. Vegetables were some form of potatoes, green beans, or corn, and a small wilted salad made up of tomatoes, cucumbers, and lettuce.

The first time I ate dinner at Susan's house, she served quinoa with almonds and dried cranberries in an acorn squash. My first meal without meat was a success. I felt cleaner and healthier.

In the coming months, I learned about tofu, and how it could be made to taste like almost anything. I ate more rice, couscous, and something called millet. During those long stretches of time when I wasn't eating with Susan, I started experimenting with black-bean and veggie burgers and steamed vegetables. Who knew that cauliflower could taste so good?

I was still eating meat, but I never felt healthy after I did.

When I wasn't making it down to Massachusetts and Susan Carter's kitchen as often, I began experimenting more on my own. I watched the documentary *Forks Over Knives* and started giving some thought to the impact my food choices were having on animals I professed to love. The film introduced me to the work that Gene Baur and his staff were doing at their Farm Sanctuary locations in New York and California. And as I read more about eating a plant-based diet, I was introduced to recipes without meat or dairy, which would have seemed impossibly foreign to me in the past.

While others might have adopted this way of eating for their health or the environment, my reason was simply compassion. After all, who was I to tell Atticus it wasn't cool for him to kill a vole while I was eating other animals, most of whom suffered during their short but hellacious lifetimes on factory farms?

One of my heroes is Dr. Jane Goodall. Her life's work with animals and her compassion for those who cannot speak for themselves and for the good earth itself often nudge me in the right direction. When she speaks, I listen, and in turn I find myself becoming more human.

In *The Ten Trusts* she wrote: "Thousands of people who say they love animals sit down once or twice a day to enjoy the flesh of creatures who have been utterly deprived of everything that could make their lives worth living and who endured the awful suffering and the terror of the abattoirs." I realized that through my ignorance and my decision not to look at what I was eating more closely, I was part of the problem she addressed.

I love animals, and yet I had done my best to ignore where the hamburger on my plate came from, the suffering of chickens that led to buffalo wings, or how many lives had to be sacrificed to fulfill my desire for barbecued ribs.

I learned something about my friends when I announced I was going to change to a vegan diet. I already knew that people like to argue about religion, politics (especially in an election year), and dogs (the right way to raise and treat them and what to feed them). Suddenly I was learning that people liked to get angry about food choices. Many I knew were mad at me for giving up meat and dairy. They attempted to shame me, and would laugh at what I was eating. I didn't mind that they continued eating steaks, chicken, and pork chops. I couldn't care less about them eating cheese and ice cream, and drinking cow's milk. That was their choice. But for some reason, they were threatened by my choice, even as I stumbled into the produce section of our local Hannaford supermarket seeking out food I'd never heard of before, such as daikon, star fruit, and gingerroot (which looks like misshapen gnomes who have been tortured into their twisted positions).

A few weeks into eating a plant-based diet, I'd lost twenty-four pounds. I'd always been a heavyset guy. Then came the next step: I chose to go on a sixty-day juice fast, the same one Joe Cross undertook when he filmed *Fat, Sick and Nearly Dead*. The extra weight melted away. I dropped from three chins to two and began sleeping through the night. My sleep apnea was gone, my skin was clearing up, my eyes looked brighter, and I was told I looked younger. My joints stopped aching; a bounce returned to my step, and I felt as if I were thirty again.

As I continued on a diet without meat, eggs, or dairy, I became more educated about what was considered vegan and what wasn't. There are phone apps for such things, one of them listing vegan junk food. When I mastered that list, I had a great time—I mean, who knew that Oreos and Twizzlers and Burger King fries were vegan?—but I gained some weight back. Then I gained a lot of the weight back. That's when I realized that eating a plant-based diet wasn't enough. Yes, I was showing compassion for animals, thinking that I wouldn't eat Atticus or Will or Aragorn, so why would I eat a cow or a pig? But cheating with junk food—vegan or not—wasn't being compassionate to me. When I understood that, I adjusted my diet again so that I was as kind to myself as I was to others.

I looked into what a vegan diet would mean for Atticus and Will. Rachael Kleidon, who is a vegetarian, used to be vegan. She had tried feeding a vegan diet to the dogs she lived with but noticed an adverse change in their health. I had my own opinion on things, but I relied on Rachael with anything that had to do with Atticus and Will. Therefore, while I gave up eating meat, they didn't.

I'm not sure I'll ever be thin, but I'm leaner and healthier. I still get tempted by the smell of hamburgers cooking when I pass a restaurant, but when that happens, I consider the animals I used to eat and how they died to make me happy. They had no joy in their lives, and most knew no freedom. They lived in fear.

And even cheese and ice cream—favorites of mine— subjected mother cows to cruelty by separating them from their calves within days, if not hours, of their birth. Long after I moved north, a farm in Newbury, Massachusetts, was in the national news because of the haunting sounds their neighbors were reporting at night, wails of sadness and heartache. People from miles around thought a cow was being tortured. It was, but not in the way they thought. Local police reported she was mourning the loss of her calf, who had been taken from her soon after its birth so that milk meant for the calf could go to people.

As part of my education, I started reading vegan cookbooks, which taught me what to eat, but also of critical importance, how to really cook. I collected so many of them that I had to buy another bookcase. Up to that point, my kitchen was home to a Crock-Pot and a George Foreman electric grill and that was about it. But as I learned to make soups and cook vegetables in other ways, I bought a pressure cooker, blender, juicer, and steamer. And I found that pancakes, muffins, bread, biscuits, French toast, and an incredible number of desserts can be veganized. Instead of using eggs, I learned to use silken tofu, bananas, flaxseed, and baking soda and vinegar.

I discovered that cooking from scratch was a lot like writing. The joy of creation goes into both, and I found contentment in the process. I was inspired by authors like Dreena Burton, Lindsay Nixon, and Isa Chandra Moskowitz. I couldn't believe how delicious the food was. And as I recently told my friend Annie Criscitiello, who is now eating in more of a plant-based way, "How can I not love the *Thug Kitchen* cookbook and the foul language used in their recipes? I'm a thug spiritualist, after all. Now excuse me while I go say my motherf'ing prayers!"

I have adapted to Will's way of living. I use my nose. I smelled celery—really and truly smelled it—and discovered its delightful aroma. I'd eaten celery thousands of times but always smothered in cream cheese, drowned in turkey soup, or used as a crunchy accent in a gooey chicken salad. But experienced on its own it was a revelation—as extraordinary as anything I'd ever eaten. Cucumbers were another, and grapes. Each trip to the produce section of a supermarket is a reawakening of my senses. The colors alone are jubilant. The taste of fresh fruit, the snap of vegetables, and the taste of nearly anything. I started taking whole tomatoes with me on a hike, and biting into them on a hot day is a sensual pleasure.

Instead of pulling into the drive-through and ordering an Extra Value Meal from McDonald's, I was stopping at farm stands and buying organic corn on the cob, lemons, peppers, apples, and bags of greens.

I found my evolution into more mindful eating equivalent to the other changes in my life, and inspired simplicity while writing or even just listening to classical music or jazz. It all wove together within me. Art became life. To cook was to write was to not just listen to the music in our home, but like Helen Keller and Will, to feel it.

The same chords were struck, the act of being present to the way my knife would slice through a ripe watermelon, the manner in which a cello rose above the other instruments in an arrangement, the way words string together to create a melody. At the heart of all of it was one seed. It was kindness. To live kindly was to live mindfully.

I don't play a musical instrument. As much as I admire those who dedicate themselves to learning the cello, piano, or violin, especially later in life, my fingers are too clumsy. They are mischievous and awkward. Some mornings I have a difficult time typing or writing letters.

It helps me to start off almost every morning by listening to Laura Carlo on WCRB out of Boston. I am a sentimental fool, and knowing that my father sat at the kitchen table with a cup of tea and a cigarette by his tinny clock radio listening to this music every day is meaningful to me. Like me, he didn't play, but classical music helped to tame the savage inside of him. It centered him. When I write while listening, I imagine I'm Beethoven, Bach, Brahms, or Mendelssohn composing something ethereal. My fingers dance across the keyboard, I pretend they are more graceful than they are, and I float into the notes, and the notes take me to the words.

When I began to eat healthier, I looked back at my relationship with fast-food restaurants and realized that no matter what I ate, I always left feeling empty inside. Making my own meals changed that, and I found a similar joy of creation out of writing. Each ingredient was a line in a poem or a note in a melody. I'm still awkward in the kitchen, but I'm getting better. The music helps as I reach for spices or a measuring cup as I will my recipes to life. There's enormous satisfaction in taking a blank page and filling it with the right ingredients to reach for a perfection I'll never grasp. The same is true of the time and attention it takes to make meals from scratch. It is another way I'm finding my religion; another way I pray without uttering a word.

Just as Will's world transformed, I was transforming my own. I started reading blogs about healthy eating, which led me to look for cruelty-free items in my choices for the bathroom. Whether it's soaps, shampoos, deodorants, or shaving creams, I choose to use products that don't put animals through testing.

Mark Hawthorne's *Bleating Hearts: The Hidden World of Animal Suffering* has found its way among the ten most important books I've ever read, and it can be found on my favored shelf not far from Emerson's *Collected Essays* or Thoreau's *Walden*. The harsh realities Hawthorne revealed forced me to see things differently. Zoos and circuses no longer seemed like fun or educational places. Instead, I saw them as the prisons they are. I'd like to think I had been kind to animals; I certainly had good standing with Atticus and Will, and different but fruitful and respectful relationships with our outside friends who spilled over from the enchanted forest on the other side of the river into our backyard fairy tale. But Mark and his peers forced me to see more, to feel more, to empathize with others I share this planet with.

My compassion for animals flows more easily than it does with fellow humans, but I am reminded once again to strive to be a better human through my relationships with nonhuman animals. The writer Ram Dass said, "We are all just walking each other home."

This brings me back to the woebegone nursing home, takes me to the present with Will, and nudges me toward a more empathetic life. How nice it is to walk a friend home. How comforting to have the favor returned.

Of course, there are always those who want to debate with me about animals and zoos and circuses and aquariums, but since my *Undertoad* days, I no longer get excited about arguing. When I'm cornered, though, by someone who insists that zoos, aquariums, and factory farms do more good than harm, I ask the simplest of questions.

"If the roles were reversed, would you be happy living in an aquarium? Do you think you could live behind bars and be satisfied in a zoo? Would you like living in the horrific conditions of animals on factory farms?"

Perhaps strangely, I have no issue with those who hunt for food. They are all around us in New Hampshire, and I have more respect for them than I had for the me I used to be who mindlessly picked through the plastic-wrapped meats at the local supermarket. But I do have a problem with trophy hunters. It's one group of people I'll never have compassion for.

I now pay more attention to the plight of such endangered species as elephants and rhinos who have been hunted almost to extinction by poachers so people can have their decorative ivory and their "medicine" from powdered horn. I am aware that human development is taking away natural habitats at an alarming rate and wiping out animals both beloved by and unknown to us.

From my life *halfway to wild,* I was understanding more about the world and drawn to the words of John Muir: "When we try to pick out anything by itself, we find it hitched to everything else in the Universe."

Atticus and I set out to find equality together while exploring life long ago. Will had grabbed hold of his chance at a new beginning. I was moving right along with them—sharing, teaching, and learning. Looking back on that time, I will always remember that the three of us were fully alive and aware of what we had during that summer of simplicity. Will and I were transforming. Atticus? I don't think he had any need to. He got it right from the beginning.

11

Thorne Pond

How beautifully leaves grow old. How full of
light and color are their last days.

—JOHN BURROUGHS

The months came and went, rushing by the way they do when contentment fills a home. Where I used to count seasons with Will, celebrating when he reached his first summer, the beginning of his first autumn, and winter's initial snowfall, I had ceased keeping track. Once Will decided to live, none of those milestones mattered any longer. What I cared about was how I filled his days.

But when midsummer of Will's third year arrived, I took note one morning as I watched him sprawled in the shade under the black ash tree. He resembled a lion in repose, proud and peaceful. The breeze stirred the grass around him, urged leaves into dancing above him, and tickled his bushy white hair. With eyes full of reborn innocence, he gazed out at his little kingdom. He looked up at me as I stepped closer. Although he couldn't hear me, and never had, I continued to talk to him.

"Do you mind if I sit down with you, Will?"

Running my fingers over his ears, I closed my eyes and tilted my head to the sky and inhaled. The hour, the day, the entire season—all smelled of singsong bliss. My spirit rocked happily along with the swaying of the leaves. Keeping my eyes closed, I listed a handful of blessings. Will was still with us. Atticus had recovered completely from his cancer. I was in good health. We had many friends and few worries. There wasn't much we wanted for. Life was as ripe as the bounty that filled the local farm stands.

Even while wrapped in that lazy happiness, though, I knew that Will was changing. He had been losing weight, becoming more frail. His skin was irritated again, breaking down beneath his fur. I had to shave ever-larger sections of it away to better treat the lesions. No matter how much ointment I rubbed on him, no matter how many medicated baths he received, or how often I washed his bedding or adjusted his diet, his skin was degenerating.

So was the rest of his body.

Will could no longer bounce around, and when he tried to ride up on his hind legs and kick out with his front paws, they barely left the ground. It was more of a windup toy kind of half hop. The gleam of life reclaimed was evident, even in his cloudy eyes, but he didn't have the energy to pull off the dance. He could still walk, but not as he used to, and I often had to carry him to his favorite places in the yard.

When I mowed the lawn, he could only feign giving chase, and I petted his head whenever I walked past him. He'd look up after me, longing to run like a rascal, but instead he flopped down and waited until I returned in the next row of neatly cut of grass.

On warmer days, I continued to take him down to the Ellis River. His trust in me was complete. I could feel it when I lifted his body, the way he sank into my arms and against my chest. He didn't mind being jostled as we walked through the woods, over uneven ground and rocks and roots obscured by the ferns. He joyfully bounced along in my arms, looking up at me.

It was always his eyes that made me smile. They'd once been narrow and suspicious, and I could tell he had stopped believing in much of anything. He didn't trust. He was in pain and looking for a reason to strike out. He had the look of a fearful soul. But as the seasons and the years passed, hope returned, and with it joy. I often thought that if he could laugh, it would burst out of him.

Down at the river, Atticus would climb onto his usual flat rock under the shade at the edge of the water and watch as I brought Will into the current. We'd sit together in the middle; no longer could he manage to sit on his own. I'd cradle him with my legs so he wouldn't tumble over. The water was warm and shallow, perfect for my old friend's weakened body. When he tired of sitting up, he'd rest his chin against one of my legs and lap the water, drinking in the lifeblood of the mountains as it flowed by us.

Those were the happiest days, but I knew they were fleeting. So I did my best to capture each moment and make it a memory, and to put things in perspective I relished how far he'd come. There was a time, back in the beginning, when I wondered if he'd last three weeks, and here he was getting ready for his third autumn.

August shuffled by. Goldenrod illuminated the deep grass that led to the forest. The leaves of the black ash began to yellow and curl. Will's wildflower garden still held some bright colors, but it was beyond its peak, with some of the older plants turning brittle. Flowers started turning to seed. The heat of earlier weeks was gone, leaving in its wake delightful days made for lounging outdoors.

In our little patch of backyard heaven, the crows watched over us, sitting up high, always chattering at Will, as if they were comparing notes about him. The chipmunks knew they had nothing to fear from Atticus, and Will had always been harmless, so they too chirped and squeaked, watching from the top of the stone wall where I gave them a handful of sunflower seeds each morning. They skittered away only when a hawk or other predator landed in one of the tall birch trees on the edge of the yard. Then they'd race with tails pointing up like furry exclamation points to whatever crevice or hole led to safety.

Aragorn ambled through on his way home at the end of many a day. He'd pause and look at us, and I half expected him to wave. Once he stopped and sat in the wildflowers, in Will's favored spot, while we viewed him from a dozen feet away. He bathed in them, smelling the dried plants around him, and then rolled over onto his back and side.

The bear and Atticus had a connection from the first day he followed us home as a yearling, but his proprietorship over

Will was altogether different. As he'd walk away toward the woods in the waning hours of light, he'd often turn before disappearing in the brush to take a final look at Will and me as we played.

I don't know if Will was ever aware of our free-to-come-and-go menagerie. He seemed oblivious to it all, other than the occasional high-pitched screech of one of the neighboring blue jays. He'd cock his head in their direction as if he was saying, *Did somebody call my name?* I imagined that without the grounding vibration of the music I played him, the few other sounds that made it through to him must have seemed like a dusty memory.

Aragorn was not the only bear to take note of the myopic little dog who took seriously his study of flowers, whether weeds or perennials. The four cubs of the Jackson Five stayed close to their mother whenever they approached from the bear path, but their curiosity got the best of them as Will circled and danced. On one occasion, they came up from behind us and startled me. Atticus and I were each sitting in an Adirondack chair while Will pranced in front of us. They walked so near that I could almost reach out and touch them, and two of the cubs lingered to watch Will's stiff pirouetting before their mother came back and nudged them along. Yet as serious as she was, she too paused to watch his dance. We all did. Even Atticus, who had so little to do with Will. He'd study his shuffle, the way he tried to leap and make his drunken circle. Will may not have been able to hear music, and his body was breaking down, but it occurred to me his life had turned into a song of rapture.

Knowing that our time together was ephemeral, I brought as many experiences to Will as possible. Atticus and I took him to Thorne Pond often in the coming weeks. Ten minutes down the road, it was an oasis for us on the days we didn't hike. We saw bear and coyote, fox and deer, and birds of all kinds, and even though ticks had laid waste to much of the moose population, I spied an occasional hoof mark in the mud. The area had the charm of its flora and fauna, but what truly captured my imagination was the mystery of this place. There in the woods, beyond the water, I never knew what would be revealed to me. Possibility permeated the land and water.

One fall afternoon, I saw Atticus looking up into a hemlock tree. Sitting on a thick branch, his arms hugging the bark, a bear was napping. I pushed Will up to where Atticus was seated. The bear, whose face was squished against the tree as he napped, opened a sleepy eye. Quickly, both eyes opened wide to assess the situation. He tensed but didn't growl. He took inventory of the three of us before surprising me by closing one eye, the one pressed against the tree. When Atticus lay down, I sat down. Will was already napping in his bedding. Slowly the bear's open eye blinked, until he fell back to sleep. Soon Atticus was napping as well, and I was the only one left awake to witness the scene. I took some photos with hands trembling in awe of the shared gentleness, until I realized nothing could capture this tableau. So I surrendered to the moment, deciding the best way to capture it was to be present.

This is what Thorne Pond came to be for us. Like our backyard, it was close to a busy road, a border between the man-made and the wild. It afforded Will an adventure a few miles away from home that wasn't too taxing for him. The trails were easy on the Will Wagon. And for me, it became a place where Mark Twain's words could spring to life: "Apparently, there is nothing that cannot happen today."

That little preserve allowed Will a glimpse through fading senses of a world that had been transformative for Atticus and me. As I pushed him along the even paths, I found myself imagining how he might have been when he was younger, and how much he would have loved cavorting in the magical forest. But I could still wheel him through it, and hope that it infused him with a grace that all living things deserve to know.

I pushed him by the sumacs, which were just turning red, and the flaming sugar maples. Always the first to change, they were a coming attraction of the pageantry that visits New England each September and October. Along the edge of the pond, Atticus and I looked down to where the lone great blue heron blended in with the rushes. Drawn by curiosity, some maturing ducklings couldn't help but follow us, paddling along in the water as we made the loop. Atticus often stopped to watch a young great cormorant who had summered there. Even though the bird was perched just feet away on a fallen tree in the pond, he was not threatened. He would even turn and look at Atticus. The two studied each other until we went on our way.

As for the heron, I'd find him following us with his pterodactyl shape as he'd fly along. So much for his shyness!

If we went in the early hours of the day, we'd spy an otter splashing as it fished for breakfast. No matter how serious his task, he always looked playful. In the evening, a family of beavers trawled the waters, coming to shore to grab a leafy shoot to munch on. They were so used to us that I was able to feed them apples, first by tossing the fruit to them as they propelled themselves back and forth, and then by hand when they eventually felt safe enough with us to come up on the grass to where we were sitting. I'd roll the apples to them until at last a bold fellow, larger than the rest, toddled up next to us and took the apple I offered him in his paws. He took a few steps away, dragging his flat tail behind him, and turned and watched us as he spun the apple in his grasp and took satisfied nibbles from it, the way I ate corn on the cob. His tiny paws, his teeth, his shining eyes, the satisfaction of eating a sweet treat—how could I not feel an affinity with him? Were we not more similar than different?

Atticus took it all in, as he always did, with a surreal tranquility, while Will sat up in his Will Wagon, seemingly oblivious to the animals we'd see. Even if he couldn't always tell what was going on around him, he was happy. It was evident in the shine in his eyes. When he was tired from sitting up, he lay down but kept his head up, as if he didn't want to miss anything.

He never made a peep unless he wanted to get out. If he was restless, he'd rock back and forth and offer up a soft whine.

I knew he could sense the plants when we circled the pond by the way he worked his nose. At one end of the loop was a great field of drying flowers and high grass. When September arrived, the sweet fragrance of decay hung in the air, and small birds feeding on the seeds would go airborne when we came too close.

We circled the smooth path around the pond so often that we became intimate with each bend in the trail, each dip and rise, the trees and brush we encountered. We knew where the birds' nests were, where the wild turkeys liked to hide, and the favored trees of the red squirrels. One bend brought us to a riot of bittersweet vines wrapping themselves around small trees and large shrubs. Their colors were a fantastic Seussical mix of neon reds, yellows, greens, and oranges. The wild tangles crowded the path and were a feast for the imagination, standing in contrast to the dying grass.

Will's nose twitched at the potpourri of the natural world. He'd close his eyes and cast his nose up to the air, savoring the coming of fall in the mountains. For all he didn't have, he seemed grateful to be outside, enjoying the temperate air and even the smell of shade that arrived late in the day when it spread across the land and the water, reminding us of the coming night.

On the far side of the pond there was a short path, fifty yards long, through dark woods down to the Saco River. We'd always look up to check the strong middle branches of the pine trees after we had startled a bear there a few weeks earlier. It was a different experience from the time we caught the previous bear napping. This bear huffed and puffed as black bears do, snapping his jaws to warn us away. I apologized for infringing on his privacy and we walked on, Atticus, me, and that little red wagon with Will in it. From that moment on, whenever we entered that path, we looked to make sure we weren't disturbing him. It's not that we were frightened; he was most likely more afraid of us. It had more to do with a kinship I felt for another who liked privacy and peace.

On the far side of that strip of woods, the trail emerged to where the Saco River passed. There was an old fallen log that had been there for years. That's where I'd sit, with Atticus in front of me, watching life flit to and fro in the trees on the opposite bank.

Will, sitting atop layers of his handmade blankets, needed his red coat, even in late summer. It warmed him and kept him from shivering. Whenever I bent over to put it on him back in the house, he graciously placed himself into position, struggling to keep his balance. Once it was on him, though, he seemed—dare I say?—empowered. He was more confident, appeared sturdier, and it let him know we were off on an adventure. After I fastened the Velcro around his waist, he'd look at me expectantly.

When summer said hello to autumn, Ken and Ann Stampfer joined us for some strolls around the pond. One afternoon, I let Will out in the meadow near the edge of the water. On the far side Bear Mountain and Mount Tremont offered a dramatic backdrop. Ken captured the early foliage and the signature scene with his camera. Eventually he turned to Will, who was stretched out on the fading grass and—much to his surprise—was watching him intently. Ken crouched down and moved closer to Will. *Click click click* went the shutter as Will batted his thick eyelashes at Ken.

Twenty yards away, Ann and Atticus were deep in conversation. Ann did all the talking, but Atticus seemed to nod along, watching every word as it left her lips. There was an understanding of sorts between the two of them. There always had been, and it stemmed from our years of hiking together. Sharing a trail brings about an intimacy found rarely in other realms. The shared struggle, the views, long miles, and long hours—you can't help but be close to those with whom you face both challenges and splendor. It is the basis of all true love.

I'll hold on to that scene forever. The four individuals I cared most about were enjoying the harmony of one another's company. The setting, the dance among them, the perfectly sunny weather. It was as good as it gets. All that love and those good hearts, in a place I was happiest. Smiles and laughter and heads nodding and twinkling eyes.

I knew to pay attention to it, because even then I understood it might never happen again.

While all of them meant the world to me, mostly I watched Will. For this was his time. This was his summit.

He had reached the mountaintop—faulty hips, poor eyesight, broken heart, immense fear, and all. He had recaptured what once was lost, and sat in that sincere place where acceptance was guiding and embracing him. He hadn't been angry in nearly two years, hadn't snapped at anyone or snarled a warning. His pain was gone, as was his lack of trust. He had come to belong, and he knew what it was to be whole.

I too had come to a time of acceptance. It spread through my body, from the tips of my fingers to the end of my toes and back up through my core. I felt it coursing through every blood vessel and nerve until it came to rest in my chest. It was a feeling of being fulfilled.

At that moment, a chill breeze stole through the forest and rippled across the water, whispering to me that the mountaintops would soon be covered in snow. For the first time I could remember, I wondered how much time Will had left.

I zipped up my jacket and pulled my Red Sox cap low on my head, making myself snug against the coming weeks. Even with that chill in the air and not knowing what we'd face, I felt blessed to have witnessed Will's journey, to have participated in it, and I knew what it meant to both give love and receive it.

Standing in that field, with the changing seasons swirling about me, I finally stumbled upon the realization that Will and I were one and the same.

Once broken, we had both come to reclaim ourselves. We each had help, but it was always our decision and our responsibility to choose to live again. No one could do that for us. It took years for me to discover where I was meant to be and where I was most alive. Will figured it out sooner than I had. He had surrendered to love and care and allowed it to wash over him like the gentle waters of the Ellis River.

Whenever people say to me, "Thank you for rescuing Will," I am heartfelt in responding, "Thank you, but he did that himself. I only gave him a place to live and helped take care of him."

And it's true. Will did the heavy lifting himself. He made the most important decisions. Whether to live or not. Whether to believe again or to forgive. Whether to love or be loved again.

Anyone who has ever been broken knows that the only one who can rescue you is the one you see in the mirror. That's why I was so proud of Will, and happy for him. When all was lost, he made a decision. It wasn't easy in the beginning, and it wasn't painless. There was suffering along the way. There always is when you learn to be vulnerable. It's a trust fall into someone's arms. A trust fall, when perhaps no one had ever been there to catch you in the past.

It takes faith. Faith takes courage.

The theologian Frederick Buechner wrote, "Faith is stepping out into the unknown with nothing to guide us but a hand just beyond our grasp."

That was Will's exercise in faith, just as it had been mine. We each left behind the sharp edges of anger, fear, and abandonment. Nothing that came before in our lives led us to believe all would be well or that we'd be safe. But there came a time when each of us had to choose to surrender to the possibilities. By surrendering to mine, I came north, and lived a fuller, richer existence. By surrendering to his, I believe Will lived longer, and he lived in love.

I'd like to say that this was my plan all along, from that May day nearly two and a half years earlier when I met Will. However, it was not. I was flying blind much of the time, trying to imagine how I would want to be treated if our roles were reversed. Talks with Marijane helped, even when they weren't about Will. My experiences in the woebegone nursing home from long ago also helped. Mostly, though, it was just looking at Will and trying to complete a puzzle that just so happened to be missing a few pieces.

What I saw in the beginning was an old fellow who was down on his luck. He needed a place to rest his head and his tired body, a place to die with dignity. Heck, I didn't even have to love him. I just needed to help him get to where he needed to be.

Fate has a way of stepping in, though. It intervenes; sometimes it shakes us until we wake up. If that doesn't work, it slaps us silly until we realize we have to open our eyes and figure things out.

In our case, fate just happened to match Will up with a fellow who had suffered in many of the same ways he had, and that jigsaw puzzle became a little easier to put together as time went on. What started out as an act of kindness turned into a spiritual journey for me. For the first time in my life, I was serving someone selflessly. Although I was not a Christian or religious, it was the most Christ-like action of my life. While bathing Will, cleaning up his urine and feces, taking care of his rotting flesh, and turning the other cheek, I felt like I was learning how to serve, much as Christ washed the feet of the apostles.

When I shared this with Marijane in the days before she died, I could sense her smile out in Phoenix. She listened intently, and finally I heard her say, "Yes. Yes, Tommy. Yes!"

Marijane had left behind her calling as a nun, but not her spirituality. She believed in holding on to yourself, but also in giving without ego. We talked for hours at a time, often several times a week. It was rarely about the mundane. It had more to do with the sacraments of living. She had been gone since the previous spring, but I still talked with her often. We were so close at the end that I had no trouble "hearing" what she would say to me whenever I posed her a question. That day in the field with Ken and Ann, Will and Atticus, maybe the wind wasn't the only thing whispering to me. For I could picture my generous aunt saying, "Will now walks in beauty."

Of course she was right. She pretty much always was.

I was merely extending the practice of what Atticus and I had learned together over more than a couple of thousand mountains. I was treating Will as an equal, and learning more about the world by experiencing things through his senses.

I'd looked at him many times a day and said some semblance of the following:

"Show me what you want."

"Tell me who you are."

"Let me help you, Will."

During our time together, we figured things out. I didn't need to love that crusty old fellow to see him to the end of his life, but he became one of the great loves of my life. While helping him to save his soul, I helped my own. Everything we did together was an act of love.

With deep October upon us, the only color remaining in the forest was that of the evergreens and the bright yellow of the enduring young beech leaves, which drop slowly throughout the winter. Everything else was gray and brown.

Will's energy dropped in unison with the hemlock, oak, and maple leaves. He couldn't get to his feet anymore without my assistance. I'd often have to hold him up to go to the bathroom. He was getting weaker and shakier and more helpless.

Will's red coat was now essential whenever we were outside. Over the course of several weeks, he had lost seven pounds. His joints were stiffer, no matter how often I massaged them and put him through his range-of-motion exercises. He stopped eating regularly, sometimes falling into his food and dropping off into a deep sleep. Increasingly, his legs gave out. He'd end up in a heap on the floor, tangled in wires or chair legs, or trip over one of his beds. He'd lie waiting for me to come and get him, his eyes drawing me closer, asking for help, full of helplessness.

One afternoon we left Will alone for only twenty minutes when we drove to the town dump with a week's worth of trash and recycling. As soon as I stepped out of the car I could hear Will crying out. Atticus and I ran up the stairs to find that he had fallen and was twisted up in the legs of a folding table. He couldn't move. His sobs reached out to me, and when I pulled him up and held him close in my arms, I felt how he trembled; his whimpers brought me to tears. Atticus approached him for only the fourth time in his years with us. As I hugged Will, Atticus pressed his head against Will's back.

That's when I knew.

That's when I surrendered yet again.

The prospect about what I was about to do both frightened me and made me strong. Whatever time remained was now Will's, and my responsibility to my friend was to be there for him.

I was about to extend to him one of the most loving things I've ever done.

I telephoned Rachael Kleidon. As soon as she heard my voice, she knew. I let her know that I wanted to be wrong. But with Will falling down countless times a day and unable to get up again, I knew. If that wasn't enough, his eyes were telling me. They were soft and devoted; there was also something more within them. I never pretend to know what someone else is thinking. However, reading Will for as long as I had, I noticed that this was a new look. He was searching my face, just as I had always searched his.

I'd like to think he was asking me a question, and wanted to know what came next.

"Rachael, he seems at peace. He's so weak, and he's suffering, but it doesn't seem to be horrific. I mean . . . I think it may be harder for me than him."

Rachael listened. In her lack of words I already knew what she was going to say. I could hear her trying to hold on to her emotions. "Tom, you know Will better than anyone. I have no doubt you are making the right decision."

We spent a few more minutes on the phone, but neither of us was able to complete our sentences. Rachael and I had lost our words; there were only feelings.

The next day Will, Atticus, and I went to Rachael's office. Will was in my arms, and she kissed him on the forehead. The way she looked into my eyes . . . there was no doubt why she was our veterinarian. She had always been a perfect match for us. Through allowing me to sit in on the amputation of Atticus's toe, to giving him chemotherapy in the office so I could be with him, to the roller coaster of Will's life, Rachael had always been the picture of empathy.

She talked about Will's weight loss, and his inability to stand or even hold himself upright when we placed him on the blanket on the examination table. She listened to his heart, and it was strong. That and his eyes were the only places where he showed his zest for life still. But even in his eyes, the flame was dwindling.

"Am I wrong?" I asked her.

"No, Tom, you're not." She reached over and gave me a hug.

"If it's okay, I want to do it the way I told you about, and I want a few more days with him if possible."

"Of course, but I prefer to do it this week. The end is going to come quickly. I don't want him to suffer any more than you do, Tom. He hasn't known that for a long time. It's one of the gifts you gave him."

It was Monday morning. "Friday . . ." My voice broke. "Friday."

"I think that's a good plan, Tom. He's right on the edge, and I think he'll be okay until then, but know I'm here for you guys if he needs to have it done sooner."

Will was getting weaker by the hour, it seemed, but he was serene. I was ready to let him go, but selfish enough to want a few more days with him.

Atticus had watched Rachael and me closely. Ever the stoic, whenever she spoke, he looked to her, and when it was my turn, he'd look in my direction. At times he looked at Will, who was now back in my arms, resting his weak head on my neck.

Back at the car, I placed Will on the floor in the back, on his bedding. Before I closed the door, Atticus did something he'd never done. He stood in my way and then hopped in next to Will. He didn't lie next to him, but sat up and looked straight ahead. Atticus had never chosen to sit in the back before, and he had almost always avoided Will.

Atticus was doing Atticus things.

I called Ken and Ann right away and let them know the news. When I mentioned what Atticus was doing, I said, "He's not looking at Will. It's like he's keeping watch over him instead." By the time I hung up on our conversation, Ken and Ann had also lost their words. I know they were mourning for Will, but their hearts were breaking for me as well.

That's the thing about those who mean the most to us. Words are not always necessary in conveying the most important things in life. Often it's the space between words that sends the message. In that pause, the sigh, the struggle to fight back a sob. We know when someone is smiling on the other end of the line. We also know when their hearts feel deeply.

In my devotion to Will over the next few days, I discovered a fresh closeness. It's something I felt when going through Atticus's cancer operation and chemotherapy. All that mattered was what existed between us. The rest of the world, all the noise, all the tears and stress, evaporated. We had entered into a sacred period of our lives, and in that acceptance of what was to be and the celebration of what had been, we were creating a sanctified place. Will had performed the ultimate trust fall, and I caught him.

I bought Will his favorite treats, played with him, held him more, and when I washed him in the tub, I felt as if I were preparing him for the mystery beyond. To be entrusted with this act of kindness empowered me. Everything we did in those closing days was a prayer. Every hug, every kiss, each time our eyes met in understanding.

I wanted Will to have more flowers, so I stopped to see Carrie and shared the news with her. Will's personal florist took it as you would expect.

Words alone can't describe what takes place when a heart aches and then breaks. But eyes tell the story, and I saw it in Carrie's.

As we left, I thought about the first time I met Carrie. Atticus and I had just moved to Jackson and we met her and Tulip, a tiny puppy she had just brought into her and her husband Joe's life. I wasn't that far removed from my Newburyport days, and my reporter filter screened everything. She was bubbly and kinder than I could believe. We talked for several minutes, and by the time we parted, I was thinking, *There is no way anyone is that nice. It has to be an act.*

Over the years, though, I learned Carrie was as pure as anyone I'd ever met. She has become a close friend.

Carrie played a real role in Will's redemption. It wasn't just that she provided flowers for him; it's as if she chose and arranged them specially to appeal to him. On the rare days I brought Will flowers from the grocery store, he was pleased, but when I bought them from Carrie, he responded strongly. He'd reach for them and want to hold them, and often I couldn't get them in water right away because he'd lay his head down on them and fall asleep.

Imagine the dreams those fragrances brought to his world. Imagine the comfort he took in falling deeply into what might as well have been an entire field of flowers.

In the few days that followed, Will was happy, but he became weaker. When I helped him stand, he did well for a few minutes, but he'd soon collapse. There was usually a period in the afternoon when he was a little bit stronger. But I was on constant call for him. I understood that's how it would be until Friday, and I welcomed being there for him, no matter how tiring it was. The one thing that convinced me that I wasn't being too selfish was how he responded. Strength may have been dwindling from his old body, but contentment remained.

To assist him, I fed him by hand, and held his water bowl for him when he drank. At night, he no longer got out of bed, so I put a diaper on him when he slept. Everything was changing except what I offered him and what he received. He continued to get fresh flowers, and there was always music. I'd put his blankets in the clothes dryer to warm them, and then tuck him in. Because he had difficulty lifting his head, I'd place a pillow under it.

Always in my head was my old contract with him: Will, you've come so far, you don't owe anything to anyone. You are free to go whenever you want, but gosh, please know that you're welcome to stay as long as you wish.

As the sand was running out of Will's hourglass, I was ready for him, as was Rachael. How special it is to be able to send someone on his way to whatever waits beyond. I was grateful to be able to make this choice for one I adored.

This had always been my responsibility to him, from the first promise I made to him on that very first day, with blood from my thumb dripping into his mouth. *We'll help you get to wherever it is you need to be.*

Will was there.

When I posted the news on our Following Atticus Facebook page, the responses came rushing like a flood. How was it possible that this lonely dog, who'd come to us without a friend in the world, now had hundreds of thousands of people mentioning him in their prayers and writing about how he had changed their lives, and openly crying at their jobs and in front of family and friends? How had this happened? He would never know these people. He knew only Atticus and me, Ken and Ann, Rachael, Carrie, Roy Prescott at the radio station, and a few others. But it seemed that the world knew of Will.

As I sat in the backyard with him wrapped up in his quilts—the crisp brown leaves blowing around us and the last of the acorns and chestnuts falling to earth, plunking through the undergrowth loud enough for me to look up expecting one of our local bears—I thought of the endless ripples his example sent forth into the world.

People were wearing "Will's Wisdom" T-shirts. They were sipping tea and coffee and hot chocolate out of "Will's Wisdom" mugs. Every penny from our portion of the sales made its way to the Conway Area Humane Society to help other homeless animals who like Will needed another chance. The echoes of his life reminded me of the glorious thunderstorms that pass over our mountains. The thunder booms so loud you can almost feel the ground shake, followed by resounding echoes that travel through the ravines and down into the valleys, and bounce off other mountains.

I knew that Will had become a hero to many who had

given up. Perhaps life hadn't been kind to them, or health was an issue. Loved ones grew old and infirm, and some died, and Will was there to lead by example. If Will could move onward, by all means, so could they.

The celebration of Will's life lasted over the course of those declining days. People we'd never met offered up kind words and tried their best to lift my spirits. But here's the thing—my spirits weren't down. I was feeling resolute. I was right where I was supposed to be, fulfilling a promise to a friend.

The Facebook posts were so impassioned, richly tender, and deeply mournful that I had to stop reading them; I needed to spend as much time with Will as I could. Still, I was glad I had shared the last few days with those who followed Atticus and Will closely. They deserved their good-byes and their heartache. When it comes to affection, I believe in osmosis. Marijane and I spoke of it often.

There may be some who are still alive but we are no longer close with for any number of reasons, or distance keeps us away from them, or circumstances. It doesn't mean we love them less, or not at all. Marijane always urged me to offer my love to those who might not be able to accept.

"Tommy, still mention them in your prayers. You don't have to be with someone to offer your love to them. Keep them warm in your heart. You will be surprised how often those feelings will find their way to them."

I'm not sure if this belief of Marijane's came from her time in the church, her years with the Navajo, or her studies of Jung. Maybe it was a combination of all three. I liked the idea of sending my highest sentiments to others with no expectation of return, so I adopted her suggestion. In my daily prayers, I name about ten people I'd like to send blessings to:

five whom I love and another five whom I might not even like. Since I believed in this kind of prayer, it was easy to share Will's last days with hundreds of thousands of people who had never met him, but felt close to him and had invested in his life.

I'd always wanted to get Will to the point where pain and fear no longer held him captive. Similarly, I wanted him to meet death as if welcoming a friend after a well-lived life. I missed Marijane something fierce in those last few days. We would have rhapsodized about the miracle of death and what brought us to this threshold. But I still talked to her, and somehow her words made their way to me. Mostly, though, it was the same message: *Will is walking in beauty.*

In the last days, Roy Prescott came over to say good-bye to Will. He lay on the floor with him and kissed him good-bye. "It's been an honor, my friend," Roy said as he wrapped his arms around him.

On the Jackson loop we ran into Kevin and Michele Pratt one last time. They were standing in front of Flossie's, their general store. She had always been kind to Will. There was something nurturing in the way Michele greeted him and spoke into his deaf ears. She stooped down until she was face-to-face with him. As I watched this heart-melting scene, I thought about how quickly our last good-bye would come.

On Wednesday, we visited the meadow at Iron Mountain. Of all the trailheads in the White Mountain National Forest, it is the most scenic, and the only one where the view from the small dirt parking lot is better than the one from the summit. From the meadow, Pinkham Notch stretches north. To the right are the Wildcats and the Carters. To the left are Monroe, Washington, Adams, and Madison of the Presidential Range, the fourth, first, second, and fifth highest peaks in New England. It's a staggering view made even better by the lack of man-made structures. Your eyes leave the meadow and travel forward to those mythic peaks as a raven would fly, over treetops, hills, and valleys, before they climb to where the natural monuments touch the heavens.

There was a trace of snow above the tree line, and working its way across a deep cerulean-blue sky was a massive lenticular cloud.

I brought my lunch and treats for Atti and Will. We climbed up on the meadow, with Will riding on my shoulder, until we had the best view possible. After eating, Atticus sat with me, regarding the numerous mountains he knew so well. Will, meanwhile, had marshaled some strength and was doing his best to walk through the grass. The ground was uneven and he stumbled, but I let him walk. He staggered away from us, catching himself when he started to wobble, making it ten yards, twenty, and finally thirty. He was wearing his red coat, and by now it was a little large for him. But he looked kingly in red, with that contrasting white color.

Will then did something new for him—something that had me fumbling for my camera. He sat with his back to us and looked out at the majesty stretching before him. I'd seen Atticus do this thousands of times. It was what the hiking community had come to know as his "Little Buddha" pose. But Will had never done it. He could never see things far away, and his sore hips made sitting difficult, especially during the last days. I was shocked he'd made it that far, yet he managed to stay upright.

Will sat for several minutes.

It was astounding to see him taking everything in. This is what I had wished for him in the days right before we met. I imagined him climbing a mountain or two with us, finding himself at the summit, sitting Little Buddha–style, and accepting the grace of where he was.

Will wouldn't see me wipe the tear from my cheeks as I picked him up and pulled him close for a hug. I carried him back to the car, and in the five minutes it took to get home he was asleep again. Dear old Will, he of the youthful soul and ancient body.

People would often say, "Will has an old soul." I disagree. His soul was shiny and new. Although I always treated him with the same dignity I offered all older beings, both animal and human, that his soul was buoyant and hopeful. Atticus had the old soul. Wise, uncanny, steadfast. What threw people off about Will was not his soul, but the body he carried it around in.

That last week, the nightly Willabies meant even more to me. I chose the songs carefully and shared nearly everything on Facebook. The photos of Will in the meadow in his kingly red coat. The Willabies. My thoughts as the hours ticked by.

When Will moved to Jackson in May of 2012, we had six thousand followers on Facebook. There were now more than two hundred thousand, and it seemed as if every one of them wanted to say good-bye. Once unwanted, Will was now the center of an expanding universe, part of the important fabric of life.

I've often thought about how people love Atticus, but it was different with Will. Atticus had a presence that was otherworldly, beyond all of us. But something about Will spoke to each and every one of us. He knew heartbreak, hopelessness, disappointment, pain, betrayal, and abandonment—the experiences we recognize in the lines of our own faces when we look into the mirror each day. We can all relate to the emptiness of going without love, understanding, compassion, or empathy. We know what it is like to be lonely or without a friend, whether for a day or a year. Atticus had never known a day without love. He was consistently self-assured, confident, with a knowingness about the world. There was no reason for him to feel any other way. No, most of us have no clue what it's like to live as Atticus lived—for his entire life.

Atticus represents an ideal, a possibly unattainable hope. Will is us, with all our fears, scars, and possibilities.

On Thursday, Carrie called to say flowers were coming for Will. When she arrived with eight arrangements, I placed them around him as he slept. When he woke up and saw the splashes of color, his eyes grew wide. He struggled to get to his feet, but in his hurry he fell. When he could stand with my help, he approached each arrangement and greeted it with deep sniffs. But try as he might, he couldn't make it to all of them before his legs gave way. One by one, I brought them before him. He was like a child on Christmas morning. If I could have that much delight in only one minute of life, I would have found something purer than anything I've ever known.

I was troubled on Thursday night. I slept on the couch, with Atticus tucked behind my knees, because Will refused to leave his flowers behind. I fought to stay awake, knowing in hours I would never have Will to sit with again. Ultimately

I failed, and when I awoke on Friday morning, rain lashed against the windows. The rain was forecasted to stop, but the day was to stay overcast and cool.

The plan was to meet Rachael at her office at eight in the morning. She was going to insert a port in Will's leg, and after work she'd drive with us to the Iron Mountain meadow where we'd say good-bye. (With the port, she wouldn't have to search for a blood vessel in the middle of a field.)

When I carried Will to her, she looked at him and her face betrayed her attempt at bravery. She said, "Tom, he has deteriorated even more in only a few days." Tears lined her eyes. "I am so glad we are doing this. But it's such a gloomy day. I just talked to Bryant, and I have tomorrow off and the forecast is for sun. Wouldn't you rather do this in sunshine, when he can see the mountains?"

Yes, yes, yes! I could have kissed the good doctor.

In some ways, I felt selfish. I was doing my best to honor my promise to Will and take whatever pain he had by making it mine. And yet when a daylong reprieve was offered, I lunged for it.

As it turned out, it was a good thing I did, for something remarkable was about to happen.

Whenever I considered the day I'd have to say good-bye to Atticus, I didn't have strong feelings about how it should go. It goes unsaid that I would be with him as he drifted off to a new world in his sleep or died in my arms, for we were always together. But how Atticus and I said good-bye ultimately wasn't as important to me as how I said good-bye to Will. Atticus had lived a full life, and had never had a reason to doubt anything. He'd known only acceptance and this tight bond. Will was different. I will never stop imagining what that night in the kill shelter was like for him. It has haunted me since the beginning. When the time came, I wanted to hold Will, and let the last thing he felt be love, and the last thing he saw be my smile and my eyes. I wanted it to happen before he suffered too much.

The rain tapered off and the sun surprised us. Since we had an extra day together, we spent as much of it outside as possible, Will in his coat, keeping him warm against the chill. We played in the backyard when he could stand, or he rode around in his Will Wagon.

Back at home, Will settled in for a nap. When Carrie called to say there were more flowers ordered for Will, I was pleased for him. When she told me how many deliveries she'd have to make, I thought I heard wrong. She and her staff delivered flowers all day long. Our living room was so full there wasn't a place to put them all.

In the previous year and a half Will had received close to two hundred arrangements from his fans. On the day before he died, our apartment was filled with about two hundred orders in one day. They came from near and far, from across the country and across the sea. People had called the little Dutch flower shop in tears, telling Carrie and her staff how much Will meant to them. It became so crazed that one person was assigned just to handle the nonstop phone calls, while extra people were called in to put together bouquets.

Will had me, and he had Atticus. But it turned out he had more friends than I ever guessed. He would actually meet very few of them, but I'd seen many of their stories on Facebook and in letters.

"If Will can do this, I can beat my cancer."

"If Will can learn to love again, so can I. I thought it was impossible after my son died."

"If Will can be brave enough to trust again, I'm going to trust again too."

People with cancer, with heart disease, with broken hearts, with disabilities, with depression—Will had them believing in themselves again. He had them believing in possibilities. Battered wives, men who'd suffered amputations. People facing terminal illnesses or who had just given up on life or love. They had all been inspired by Will.

One of my favorite stories came from Ann Marie Buttaro.

"I was ready to give up on love. I had been married and divorced, and my children were grown. I had a few relationships but for one reason or another they didn't work out. I thought I was content to stay single for the rest of my life. But then I read Will's Wisdom: 'It's never too late to trust again, to love or be loved again; and it's never too late to live again.' So I decided to try again. We met on an online dating site. I liked his photo by accident. I think God had something to do with that! Now we are married. Thank you, Will, for showing me it's never too late!"

There were those who had been in despair, laid off after thirty years at the same job, and were looking for the courage to chase new dreams. Some people with agoraphobia swore Will gave them the courage to give the world another chance, and they went back to school or expanded their world socially by joining clubs, going to museums, or becoming part of hiking groups. Women betrayed by cheating husbands could relate to what happened to Will. They swore it was time to love again, or at least open their hearts to it.

These sentiments made their way onto the cards attached to all the arrangements.

There were vases on the floor, the ottoman, the coffee table, the large armchair, and the couch. There were so many flowers I had to put them on the windowsills, and they spilled into the kitchen, the bathroom, and the bedroom. When Carrie called to say she was almost out of flowers, I said, "Thank goodness, because we have no more room!"

But the calls kept coming. People wanted to say thank you and good-bye to Will.

Looking at her bare glass flower cooler, Carrie told them she still had some roses left. If they wanted to, they could order a single long-stemmed rose for Will, and her staff would attach a note to it. That was the biggest vase of all. I'm not sure how many roses there were, but it seemed like more than fifty.

Watching those flowers come for a little dog who couldn't see well, couldn't hear in the least, had lost his appetite, and was so weak he could barely stand, I thought of the pleasure he'd receive with his wondrous nose. As I placed the bouquets around the apartment, I reminded myself that it doesn't matter where or what you come from, it's how you end up. Here was Will, that shelter long forgotten, his abandonment erased, warmed by quilts made just for him and by the sunshine reaching through the picture window to caress him. He was surrounded by an ocean of color and fragrance that could only seem like heaven on earth. This was what he had made of his life. This was his Beethoven's Ninth Symphony, his "Ode to Joy"!

Will continued to sleep as the flowers made their way into our home. He was covered up and snoring soundly, completely unaware of that exclamation of love awaiting him. I had to leave a path to his bed, but it was very narrow in order to fit everything in. When he awakened, he trembled at the scent. He tried to stand, but his blankets weighed him down. I peeled them off him and helped him up. His rear legs shook with the effort as he craned his neck to reach into his private garden. He fell, tried to get up. I helped him stand again. With shaky legs he made his way down the garden path. He looked all around him, and when he paused too long or reached out too far with his nose, he fell again. He struggled to get up, and I kept helping him. When he tired, he lay down. Even then he tried to crawl across the floor to get closer to all those visitors who had come to say good-bye to him. His eyes were vibrant, brilliant, and alive.

Twice he fell asleep, and I covered him.

Before the sun went down, I took him out for another loop in the Will Wagon. Cars pulled over and people got out with tears and handkerchiefs to say farewell. Many of the people of Jackson had opened their hearts to him from a distance, and this was their chance to say good-bye. The town never felt more special to me than it did on that day. We finished our walk with one last visit to Dutch Bloemen Winkel. Carrie and her staff were exhausted. Every bouquet for Will had been created as if it were the only one; no two were the same. All the flowers were gone, and still the phone kept ringing.

When we returned home, Will and I were exhausted.

We slept through the night, a rarity in those last days, and when I awakened, I looked over the edge of the bed, just as I had done every morning since he came to live with us. There was Will, just as I had left him.

When Atticus and I entered the living room, I'd almost forgotten the flowers were there. I took time to read several cards. Each sentiment was unique. The feelings expressed were genuine and heartbreaking.

But as uplifting as it was to feel the love Will had been blessed with, I could feel the melancholy sneaking up on me. We were down to our last hours together.

The day before, the world had had the opportunity to say good-bye to dear Will. This day belonged to me and to Atticus.

I never expected Will to live so long. I couldn't fathom that I would love him as much as I did, especially not after those first months. I had Atticus in my life, and he had always been enough. He and I were just doing an old dog a favor at the end of his life. It was an act of charity.

When Will didn't get out of bed, I went looking for him. He was awake but he couldn't get up. I greeted him with cheer and carried him outside. As it was in the beginning, it was in the end: I had to hold his hips up so that he could go to the bathroom and not fall in it.

My heavy heart aside, the day couldn't have been any more pleasant. It was as picturesque as a postcard, with a dazzling sky and warm sunshine. Thank goodness for Rachael's suggestion to wait. Will would go to the meadow and the mountaintops beyond on a perfect day.

The scent of midautumn greeted us for our last loop around town. At the gazebo by the Wildcat River across from the post office, I took Will out of his wagon and let him walk around as best he could. He didn't last long, but before he settled down like a lamb, he shuffled up to Atticus and the two touched noses. They held each other's eyes until Will's legs gave out. In that silent moment, there was more being said, I believed, than I would ever know.

Rachael met us at our house and we sat in the backyard talking about chipmunks and bears and Wildflower Will's garden. As we played with Atticus and kept Will close, the old fellow just looked tired. He had nothing left.

"You okay?" Rachael asked.

"Yeah, I'm being brave." I smiled. "I feel okay."

"You're doing the right thing, Tom. Please know that. You've always done right by Will and Atti."

"I know . . . I know . . ."

From the meadow, the mountains were resplendent. I carried Will up the hill in the first prayer shawl that was made for him. It came from Lisa Money down in North Carolina, and it was as red as the rose I carried with us. Rachael and I were silent. Atticus led the way. He had been up this path many times, rarely stopping at the meadow, and almost always climbing to the top of the mountain, even under the stars on the nights we couldn't sleep. When we found a level, comfortable spot, we all sat together. We fed treats to Will and Atticus. When Will couldn't keep himself upright, Rachael tucked her jacket behind him. There was music and laughter and kisses. It was as light as love.

After a long while, Rachael said, "Are you ready for the first injection? It will just make him sleepy."

I held him in my arms, wrapped in his handmade blanket and with his rose under his nose, when she attached the needle to the port. He looked up at me and I smiled down at him.

"I'm here, Will. I love you. Thank you for everything, my friend."

It didn't take long for sleep to take over his body. His

familiar snores rose up to greet us. They were so loud we couldn't help but smile through the weight of our hearts. I placed my phone on his chest and played some of his Willaby songs.

Twenty minutes later Rachael asked me. "Okay?"

"Yeah, okay. But let me stand up first."

When the second needle went into the port, it was almost instantaneous. Will grew light, and for that split second I wanted to pull his life back to me. But it was gone, and I felt it leave. He was gone.

I asked Rachael and Atticus if I could have a few moments alone with Will. They stayed back together, Atticus sitting and watching me carry Will toward the mountains in the distance.

I walked halfway across the field cradling Will in my arms. I let out a primal wail that echoed in the ravines and across the mountaintops. It was as wild as the landscape. His pain had become mine.

There Will and I stood, right where I wanted him to be when we said good-bye, under the watchful eyes of Agiocochook and Passaconaway.

I brought him out to the place where he sat down a few days ago, so the mountains could see him, I told myself.

I squeezed the vessel of that body I knew so well against my chest. I wanted it to feel my heart beat. I wanted Will to feel my love for him, and how proud I was to be part of his journey. Finally I raised him above my head in that October meadow and asked the mountain gods to look after him.

"He is yours now. Please take care of him. I have loved him like no other."

When I turned to walk back to Atticus and Rachael, I

pulled Will's ear against my mouth and I whispered some words I borrowed from William Butler Yeats.

> I would ride with you upon the wind,
> Run on top of the disheveled tide,
> And dance upon the mountains like a flame.

Rachael offered to take Will's body back to the hospital by herself, but I said we were also going.

"Do you want me to take Will in my car?" she asked.

"No, I've got him."

How could I let him go? We'd been together since that day in Connecticut, and I was not yet ready to say good-bye. I had delivered his soul to the place where it was meant to be, and now I would see his body to the very end. In those ten miles from the meadow to North Country Animal Hospital, I drove with Will cradled in my left arm. I kissed him a hundred times, at least, and wanted to kiss him a hundred more.

I was shattered. My soul was split open and rebuilt all at once. I was empty, I was full. I was half dead and completely alive. Both tired and awake, confused and clear. It wasn't just from the day, it was for all of Will, and all of me.

I can think of no greater gift than to help someone regain who they are. To guide them until they find their way again, and remember who they were meant to be. That's what we did with Will.

Just as when I had held a lonely alcoholic man during his dying hours, I could feel the miracle of Will's soul depart. The lightness of the body that once confined him. I pictured him perhaps being reborn as a puppy or a bear cub or a chipmunk, and see him playing, running without bad hips, seeing the stars with clear eyes, hearing the wind and the birdsong.

Whenever a friend experiences the death of one they love, and words are hard to come by, I ask them, "What does your faith tell you? What do you believe? This is when it matters most. This is when faith takes over."

That night, back in our apartment, sitting with Atticus and surrounded by Will's flowers, but without Will for the first time in nearly two and a half years, I asked myself the same question. *What does my faith tell me?*

I believe that the soul doesn't die. It is permanent. Not just on this plane, but on other planes as well. And I believe that my life goes on as well, carrying forth the gifts Will and I had exchanged.

For I believe.

Yes, I believe.

12

Beech Leaves

Some nights in the midst of this loneliness I
    swung among the scattered stars at the end of
    the thin thread of faith alone.
—WENDELL BERRY, *Jayber Crow: A Novel*

I n Japanese, the word *kintsukuroi* means "to repair with
gold." It is the art of mending broken pottery with gold or
silver lacquer and understanding that the piece is more valu-
able for having been broken. What once was ruined forevermore glitters and glows at the broken places.

Whenever people talk to me about how Atticus and I res-
cued Will, I tell them it was an inside job. Psychology 101
tells us we cannot rescue anyone but ourselves. You can help

someone out of a deep, dark hole, but the rest of it us up to them. All the credit for Will's rescue goes to him. We offered him hope, a home, some help along the way, but what he did with it was out of our control.

This is the core of Will's story, his choice to live again. He made it that morning he crawled to my bedside after those first weeks, and he made it every day after that. I'll never underestimate the courage that took. Looking at his various beds around the apartment, listening for snores I would no longer hear, thinking about how I would finally be able to sleep through my nights without a bell ringing or having to give him a surprise bath, I was exhausted. More important, though, I felt reverential.

It's nice to think that love can conquer all. It's a Hallmark sentiment, and it may offer hope to the hopeless. But for those of us who have loved and lost, it doesn't ring true. I have loved people in the past who were too broken, too far gone, to live again. They crawl into a bottle or take pills or get lost in anger. I have known some animals who were the same way. They couldn't remake themselves. They couldn't rise above their bitterness or what humankind had done to them. A fresh start was not possible, and opening their hearts again was not realistic. They were simply broken to never be made whole again.

Love offers us her gifts, but she must be met somewhere in the middle with courage and faith. That's part of Will's legacy. He didn't give up when he had every reason to do so.

Life can be so many heavenly things, but it can also be violent and savage and thoughtless. So how do we fix it? How do we mend the broken and make someone or something whole again? I'm no expert—I still reach out in the darkness for that hand just out of sight—but I've grown to believe it has to start with us. We fix ourselves, and when we are ready, we try to help others. We never rob them of their journey, their experiences—the ones that help define who they are. Some treks up the mountain have to be made solo. But you never know when a helping hand or a cup of coffee or a smile will feed a starving soul.

One of Will's gifts was helping me to remember what it meant to be gentle. I can be loud and coarse, witty and cutting, strong and obtuse. I can be a bull in a china shop. Like all of us, I've been broken into bits and pieces, but I choose to move on and believe. Will had me practicing gentle, empathetic ways.

Rarely did I ever say, "Poor Will."

It was more important to put myself into his place than to look down upon him. If anything, I'd say, "Tell me what hurts." I never really cared what had happened to him. I was more focused on what we could do to help him move forward.

In the days after Will died I read books that helped me make sense of my emotions. Poetry, theology, and mythology. I turned to a dog-eared paperback copy of Joseph Campbell's speeches and essays. I kept returning to the same passage that reflected his interview with Bill Moyers on PBS. Moyers asked him about the meaning of life, and Campbell responded that we're not looking for the meaning of life but for the experience of being alive.

To give your heart, to have it filled and renewed, knowing all the while it will one day break again because of that love—it's all part of the experience. Vulnerability is a necessary component of love.

On the night Martin Luther King Jr. was assassinated,

Bobby Kennedy spoke in front of a crowd of African Americans who didn't yet know of King's murder. He spoke with grace and eloquence. Among his words: "And let us dedicate ourselves to what the Greeks wrote so many years ago: to tame the savageness of man and make gentle the life of this world."

Will was my lesson in gentleness, even when he was fighting me and his teeth ripped into my flesh. It was a lesson in humility and kindness. I came to him unarmed, time and time again. After several months, he realized he no longer had to attack. My gift to him was patience. His gift was helping me evolve beyond the man I used to be.

H ours after saying good-bye to Will, the sun set, shadows grew tall in our backyard, and darkness spilled in through the windows. Our Facebook page was as lively as an Irish wake as I learned more about the measure of Will's influence. More than two hundred people informed me that they had adopted elderly dogs because of Will. Others had fostered them until they found a home. With that same hope of helping animals in need, I posted a link to a memorial fund in Will's name at the Conway Area Humane Society website. Within five minutes, the site crashed when twenty-seven thousand people tried to donate at the same time. That's when the first tears fell for me that day. There was no sadness, but joy. Will had truly lived—and touched the lives of others.

I spent an hour making phone calls consoling friends around the country who I knew were struggling with his death.

I was numb in the days that followed. I couldn't bear to read the thousands of sympathy cards that were sent in Will's memory. They contained too much sadness. I didn't want to be sad; I wanted to breathe and find peace.

Will's redemption was too much for me to grasp while it was going on. But in hindsight it was as close to a religious experience as anything I've ever known. Several walks a day with Atticus resuscitated me. The forest welcomed us home, and we were able to hide from society, the e-mails and the phone calls and Facebook posts. I was thankful for the kindness, but mostly what I craved was silence.

In our solitude I truly grasped that Will and I would forever be intertwined—not only with the rest of the world, but within me.

That's how I measure how important something is. I look ahead to when I'm on my deathbed, and if something is important enough, if it has touched me with profound intimacy, I believe it will float to the surface when I'm preparing to die. When that time comes, I know I will be visited by memories of Will.

But for now the days of mourning rolled together. Hours meant nothing. Having gone without a full night's sleep for most of the past eighteen months, Atticus and I went to bed early. Sleep opened its arms and welcomed me home. We'd be in bed by seven and sleep for twelve, thirteen, even fourteen hours.

The quieter I was, the more my friends worried. I assured them that all was well, that I had just been through something I've never encountered before. They didn't believe me when I reported that I wasn't depressed, I wasn't crying. They pushed and pushed for me to say how I was, and eventually it hit me that what I was feeling was humility. I had been humbled by my time with Will. It wasn't impossibly difficult to deal with his death, because death doesn't frighten me. What I mourned was the end of the physicality.

When I thought about Will, I celebrated his life. We should all be so lucky to go out on top. He was loved, and he left hearts heavy with memories and lives inspired by his tenacity. Yes, I was humbled to be part of his story.

Atticus remained his constant self. It was as if Will had never existed. Knowing him well, I expected that from him. I was the one who needed to recover. Methodically I made my way through our home, throwing out what we no longer needed and removing all the roadblocks I had put up to keep Will from getting stuck in corners and cubbyholes. I washed his things, neatly folding his blankets after they came out of the dryer. I laid them one on top of another, with the same light touch I used to lay them on top of him. Even that simple act was a prayer.

I knew what I'd do with all of those blankets and quilts. Will had awakened something in me, and I'd long been thinking that I wanted to help others like him. But not just dogs and cats—all animals. A vision came to mind of a small farm, one I can handle mostly on my own, where neglected and abused animals can come to reclaim themselves. I picture a couple of donkeys, some pigs and cows, sheep and goats. I envision a farm for lost causes, where there will be music and laughter and Will's blankets and patches of wildflowers and sweet william planted wherever joy is needed. It will be a place of tranquility, and the elderly from local nursing homes will be invited to sit with the animals, feed them, pet and touch them. I also see raised gardens they can tend without bending too much or getting out of their wheelchairs, where they can watch the cycle of life play out by the seasons.

Oh, and those goats and those sheep won't be treated as goats and sheep, nor will the donkeys and pigs and cows be treated like donkeys and pigs and cows. Like Atticus, like Will, they will be treated as individuals. They will be as equal to me as I am to them. Call it a transcendental farm if you will. Thoreau and Emerson would have been pleased by the concept.

One day I hope to have the money to do this. When I wrote about it on my Facebook page, many of Will's fans offered to contribute. I was thankful, but I didn't want to take their money. There was something else that had me putting it off as well. Atticus had always had me to himself, and he had sacrificed much with Will in our lives. I would like to see what he would do with all those animals who needed to find themselves again, because I understand his ways with troubled souls. But I also knew that for a while at least, Atticus needed it to be just the two of us again.

With Will's blankets put away and the house back to normal, there was one last thing to take care of.

Will's skin festered with infection no matter how often I bathed and medicated it. One morning, when the sky was gray and cold, and I could feel winter approaching, I washed Will's red coat. When I pulled it out of the dryer, I didn't know what to do with it. I sat down numbly and held it in my hands.

There was no collar or harness, there were no tags. Whenever Will received any of the necessary shots from Rachael, she'd hand me the proper tags and laugh when I turned and tossed them into the trash with a perfect arcing shot.

There wasn't even a name tag to hold on to, or else I would have put it next to Max's on my key chain.

There was only Will's red coat.

I sat with it, holding it in my hands as if I were holding Will himself. A gentle smile came over me. Some laughter too. My chest felt warm, and my hands tingled when I moved my fingers over the soft material.

A simple coat was part of his transformation. It was for him a superhero's cape. It kept him warm, it made him feel safe. It was his signature, even when he began to shrink inside of it.

With Billie Holiday's voice filling our home, I went to the tool drawer in the bathroom and gathered a few things. Atticus followed me into the writing room, and above that old scratched and scarred Mississippi desk, I attached a large brass hook to the wall. With reverence and gratitude, I hung Will's coat from it.

At more civilized times in my life, the Novembers I'd known had felt like loneliness. They sat hollow between the vivid colors of October and the Currier and Ives charm of December. The lonely trees, the way the night steals the daylight, and overcast days have always conspired to remind me of the empty moments of my life.

When Atticus and I took to the forest, though, my feelings evolved. The trails are quietest in the eleventh month. Mountains stand naked before us. There is a bare-bones feel to them. It's more intimate. You can see far off into the distance where leaves once blocked your view. Rivers and streams run cold and clear. The sylvan floor is scattered with old leaves, like memories ready to be picked through.

November has its own smell, a cornucopia of dried fruits and berries, acorns, and chestnuts. Even the desiccated leaves give off a scent that can elevate any day. If you are still, you can even hear November's song. I used to think of the sigh and cry of the wind through the naked trees as ghostly, but it feels like a welcoming chorus to those of us who have grown comfortable with things at their most basic.

I also think of a certain leaf that remains behind after the others have fallen: the beech leaf.

Each spring beech leaves shoot out from their buds with a graceful curve. If you are watching for them, you can't miss their entry into the world. They are like decorative sabers. But soon they're swallowed up in the frenzy of late spring as leaves from maples, oaks, hemlock, and birch burst forth. The beech leaves of June are soon anonymous, lost in the uniformity of late spring, and remain that way throughout the summer and into fall. When early October arrives, most trees reveal their individuality with festive ornamentation. But the beech is still an afterthought. Then, when age and wind and rain rob the painted ladies of the woodland of their finery, something splendid is again revealed. The young beech leaves remain, glowing with a lustrous yellow that is surreal.

Even as they fade, they cling, steadfast, to youthful branches. Some will tumble through a spiral down to the ground, but most hang on, resolute, a spot of bright color in a world of black and white.

They vibrate in the breeze, sometimes only one leaf at a time when its relatives remain still, as if some tiny fairy is dancing upon it. And when the wind picks up, they whistle through its rush. In midwinter they turn a soft gold, then a papery white, until at last, before falling in spring, they're as fine as worn parchment. One April day they are there; the next, they are gone, as new buds push them earthward.

They remind me that sometimes you have to be very old to be noticed. We don't all flower at the same time. Ever since his first winter with us, I've thought of Will as a beech leaf. Anonymous, perhaps even forgotten for many years, he was at his brightest in the winter of his life. In old age's dying light, he glowed.

As I kicked through the fallen leaves with Atticus that November, the beech leaves were more luminous than I had recalled. I often stopped to trace my fingers over them and their tiny veins, to say hello and thank them for their luster.

I understand that my feelings for November are not universal. Some suffer from seasonal affective disorder and crave the sun of Florida. Some despise the cold. But step away from the malls and the coffeehouses, wrap yourself in your warmest sweater and hat and gloves, get in your car, and drive to a quiet spot where deer roam free. Spend enough time in the quietude, listen to your heartbeat and your breath, and you will no longer fear November.

Perhaps you will even come to relish the cycle of life. Yes, some plants have gone to sleep and some have died, but they've left something extraordinary behind. Their seeds are everywhere. In the drear sits the hope of new life, even if we overlook it. The cycle continues ever onward.

When I published the *Undertoad*, I had an important mentor in an elderly fellow named Doug Cray. He was gentle, thoughtful, and at times stubborn. Doug was a retired reporter who'd worked for various newspapers and magazines. His claim to fame, although I'm not sure he saw it this way, was covering Kennedy and Johnson during their terms in the Oval Office. Nothing against the late presidents, but he was more a fan of the jazz greats and would often recount his times with them.

Doug was forever writing me notes, and he signed off on most of them with the words "Onward, by all means." It was his way of urging me forward to fight for what I believed in. He was telling me, *Keep going, no matter the obstacles ahead.*

When someone who is dear to me dies, I try to incorporate something about that individual into my life. After Doug passed away, I was comforted by his signature line and chose to use it in my own correspondence.

Through the years it has become a rallying cry for Atticus and me. When facing a steep section of trail and unsure of how we were going to approach it, I'd turn to Atticus and say, "Onward, by all means, my friend." It worked when Will came along with his endless hurdles too, and when Atticus was battling cancer and the draining effects of chemotherapy.

In the face of all the death we see in November, and with frozen December approaching, all those seeds scattered across the forest floor are nature's way of saying, "Onward, by all means."

The day after Will died, I asked Carrie to come by and pick up nearly all those flowers people had sent to Will. They were still beautiful and fresh, and I wanted them to continue spreading joy elsewhere. She gladly took them to local nursing homes for those who needed them most.

I asked her to leave behind the giant vase of roses.

As October flowed into November, I took a single rose each morning to Thorne Pond and the Saco River. I would read the attached card, then drop the rose in the river and watch it be swept away. I did the same each afternoon out back in the Ellis River. Atticus sat on his usual rock as I hopped from stone to stone until I balanced in the middle of the river and let the current take the rose down to the Atlantic.

As November came to a close, I took the last rose with me and stood on my stone. The air was crisp, and a little ice clung to some of the rocks. Atticus watched and listened as I read the last card: "Will, I will never forget you. Theresa August, Phoenix, Arizona." The dried flower sailed through the air, and when it hit the water I watched it float gracefully away. I followed its course until my eyes came to Aragorn on the other side of the river. He sat watching us, just he had that day earlier in the year in our backyard. I nodded to him.

The three of us considered each other as friendly neighbors do. When I could no longer see the rose floating downstream, Atticus and I turned and headed through the brush and up the hill to our home. It was the last time we'd see Aragorn that year.

When do you lose someone forever? When are they really gone? I'm convinced it happens when they are no longer in our hearts. I knew Will wasn't walking with us, but I also knew he was there. The last rose may have floated out of sight, but that little white dog never will.

Just as I took Doug Cray's words and made them my own, I carry Will's resilience and his reclaimed innocence in the words I refer to as Will's Wisdom.

> It's never too late to trust again,
> to love or be loved again,
> and it's never too late to live again.

13

Onward, by All Means

> You do not need to know precisely what
> is happening, or exactly where it is all
> going. What you need is to recognize the
> possibilities and challenges offered by the
> present moment, and to embrace them with
> courage, faith and hope.

—THOMAS MERTON

It's a year to the day since we said good-bye to Will in the Iron Mountain meadow, under the watchful gaze of Passaconaway and Agiocochook. I think about him every day. It's always with a smile. His bright eyes; his bouncy, drunken trot; his red coat. There is no sadness. When there are tears, they are because of what we accomplished together. I find myself saying to him, "We did it. We really did it!" Long after those words are spoken, the smile remains.

It's my favorite time of the year, when the leaves have fallen, except for the beech leaves. This is their moment, and even as they fade, they still remind me of all that is beautiful and possible. Of course they also remind me of him. I no longer consider them beech leaves, but Will leaves.

On our walk at Thorne Pond today, we brought apples to feed the beavers. Atticus and I sat together as they swam up to us. Earlier in the year the young ones were skittish and would slap their tails at our passing, warning us away. But now they realized we were not a threat. They climbed up and sat with us as I rolled apples to them.

From there we stopped off at the long band of milkweed pods. They had been opened for a long time. Some still had their seeds, and I collected them in a small bag to bring home and plant in Will's wildflower garden and watch them grow in the spring. They draw monarch butterflies, who need all the help they can get, as humans have poisoned their food supply with pesticides.

When we walked down one of the paths that took us into the belly of the forest, I heard a gunshot in the distance, in the hills beyond. It's bear-hunting season. I thought of Aragorn and prayed he was okay.

The other day a local hunter created quite the outrage in the valley when he killed the mother of the Jackson Five, leaving the maturing cubs to fare on their own. These were not the cubs that used to watch Will, but a second set from the same mother.

Atticus was happy, although his hiking days were behind

him. We still got out for two or three woodland walks a day, each at least a mile. He was in good shape, although he was half deaf, and his eyes had difficulty in the contrast between the bright sun and shadow. But we were grateful for what we continued to have. Once in a while we'd climb a simple hill with a view that was made to fill the heart, but I'd tell people when they asked, "He's retired."

When they ask how many mountains he's been on top of, I have to admit I don't know. It is anywhere between two and three thousand. I stopped counting long ago. As it turns out, it was never the numbers that mattered.

Since Atticus doesn't hike anymore, neither do I. I'm sure I will again one day, but not now, not while we are still sharing our lives. Hiking was always something we did together.

I miss it, and I wonder if he does too. He still likes to be active. He's not a big fan of sitting around our home. He looks at me while I'm at my writing desk, and sits and stares until I say, "Okay, you want to go out?" He can't always hear the words these days, but just as I did with Will, I continue to say them. He responds more to my actions. The moment I turn in my seat, he hurries to the back door. It's good to see so much life left in my friend.

At night, I dream of the mountainsides and mountaintops we've climbed. In the midst of an afternoon walk, I follow Atticus down a trail, and there is something bittersweet about how many times I've followed him before. I think of pushing through the wind and temperatures below zero on Franconia Ridge, or stepping from the trees onto to that stone stage on Mount Garfield that looks out on the Pemigewasset Wilderness. I remember days we were so cold that our gear froze, and how we had to keep moving on winter hikes so that he could stay warm. The memories of all those peaks return to me, even as we make the most of our current days. When I miss them too much, I take heart in knowing that every one of the mountains we've climbed is a part of us.

When someone asks me to name a favorite hike, too many come to mind, but there's one specific route I think of that changed everything for us.

It was a June day during our second year of hiking when life was still hectic, but getting ready to change. Atticus still wore a collar, I owned a newspaper, and we lived in the red-brick city. It was before the bears and the little white dog and the cancer came. I didn't know it then, but we were on our way to finding simplicity.

We started just after sunrise, pulling into the Oliverian Brook trailhead. Within minutes, I had taken the bike from the rack on the Ford Focus and we were headed three miles up the road through the chilly air.

The only traffic was two logging trucks coming in the opposite direction. The truckers gave us a surprised double take. At that quiet hour one expects to see moose and bear along the scenic two-lane Kancamagus Highway, but I'm sure they didn't expect to see a little dog sitting in a basket attached to handlebars, looking relaxed and self-assured, his ears flapping out to the sides and behind him, and a heavy man pedaling madly uphill while wearing a backpack.

We left the bicycle chained to a tree, and Atticus watched me when I started the stopwatch on my wrist. "You ready?"

He turned quickly, bounding eagerly up the Pine Bend Brook Trail.

Birds sang to one another of our passing and we welcomed the early-morning scents of the forest—fresh and sweet, musky and earthy. The deep green leaves of late June spread out like the ceiling of a cathedral with a backdrop of a pale blue sky, while undergrowth sprouted from the ground along the sides of the trail.

We had been on the same trail before, more than once. But this time would be different. We wouldn't just climb to the summits of North and Middle Tripyramid, two of New Hampshire's forty-eight 4,000-foot mountains, and then return. We'd continue on to trails we'd never been on, including one that hardly anyone ever traveled.

We were heading into the heart of the Sandwich Range, a mystic and fantastic place, even by White Mountain standards.

The main attraction of most of these hikes is not some awe-inspiring view over miles of blue-green mountains, but those along the trail into the forests along the way. Walking in the Sandwich Range is like being in the belly of a beast, both dark and shadowy. You linger. You watch and listen.

Then you are transported.

One minute you're in your car, the next you're walking through an airy wooded glen, but suddenly—and you don't always realize when it happens—you find yourself in a fairy tale. This is the wilderness of Tolkien's Middle Earth and Lewis's Narnia. You lose yourself along challenging paths cluttered with large rocks and half expect to take a turn onto a steep trail crisscrossed by slick, spidery roots and lined by lush green moss, only to come face-to-face with a wood elf or dwarf. Mystery hides in the shadows and fertilizes the imagination. Even the birdcalls are haunting.

So it was with us that day. We hopped from rock to rock over the brook, crossing it several times as it wove its way into the valley. Through spruce, hemlock, and birch we climbed, along a trail that grew steeper and more rugged, up through a ravine, taking careful steps, always under a canopy of green. We stopped and drank water often. I fed Atticus treats when we sat together on rocks ancient and cool.

Four miles in, we reached the top of North Tripyramid. Less than a mile later we took a break on the summit of Middle Tripyramid. From there it was new territory for us, at least several miles of it. We crossed over South Tripyramid and descended a short way along its rock slide, where I wrestled with my fear of heights. I felt sure that I would tumble down the mountain. Atticus went first, stopping often to check on me. Then came the refuge of the seldom-traveled Kate Sleeper Trail. I gladly left the open air to duck into the gloom.

Of all the trails we've been on, this is my favorite. You are more likely to see a moose than another hiker. The forest is thick and primeval. It feels as though it is watching you pass through its hallowed hall. We came to an occasional fallen tree and had to find a way around it, but mostly we walked on a carpet of red pine needles, soft enough to sleep on, and through a corridor of verdant ferns.

We left the main trail for short side trips to the summits of West and East Sleeper, two viewless peaks just over 3,800 feet high. Weaving through the wooded labyrinth, I could at times look off through the woods and see blue sky beside me, but not overhead.

For two and a half miles, we traveled through the quiet and stillness with few ups and downs, and I lost myself in the movement. It was somewhere in the middle of these high woods that I realized something wasn't right. I stopped and sat on a log. Atticus trotted back to me. He looked at me expectantly.

"You want some water?" I held it out for him, but he didn't even look at it. Instead, he kept his dark eyes on me, his white eyebrows occasionally moving up and down. I looked around us, felt the forest and the way it seemed to be welcoming us.

"I'm fine, my friend. At least I will be."

I looked at my watch one last time, then took it off. I had worn it on every hike we'd ever been on so that I would know how long each trip would take us. But while sitting high in the Sandwich Wilderness with no sign of man other than the rustic trail, it seemed out of place.

I felt like tossing the watch into the woods and letting nature have its way with it, someplace where no one would ever find it. But even if I was the only one who ever knew where it lay hidden, I would still know that I'd done something unworthy of the mountains. I slid it into a pocket on my backpack and never took it out again. Not that day, nor any day since.

"Atti, come here, please."

He took a few steps closer. We looked into each other's eyes as I took off his collar. We had stopped using a leash long before then, but for some reason I'd kept his collar on. Perhaps it was for convention, or social politeness. But if I was to feel free, so was he.

From there, our traverse was joyously mindful. I stopped to feel the pinecones on the trees and bent over to do the same with the pine needles on the ground. I let my hand rest on the tree bark and imagined the life coursing through and beneath it. For the first time on a hike, we were taking our time. I even stopped to look at the frequent piles of moose droppings, hoping we'd encounter a large bull with antlers beyond measure.

When we reached a junction to the Downes Brook Trail,

we started climbing again and came to running water, where Atticus stopped. He sat and drank and watched the shimmer on the rocks. When he turned to me, I sat with him and we stayed there for a spell.

We stopped again, a mile later, when we reached the ledges of Whiteface, another four-thousand-footer. We soaked in the sun and the views, sat and enjoyed our lunch. We even shared some of it with a red squirrel who nervously peered out at us from a small tangle of weather-beaten brush. I tossed him some granola. He watched us, and ever so cautiously he took some, then scampered away, only to return for more. It took a few minutes, but he started eating out of my hand. His little fingers grabbed hold of mine and he held on while he dipped his head into the cereal. He'd sit back up and chew with his eyes watching both Atticus and me, but not fearing us.

After lunch, we did something we'd never done before on a hike. I placed my backpack under my head, stretched out, and took a nap. Atticus laid his head against my leg, under some shade, and did the same. When we awakened, the little red squirrel was watching us. I said good-bye, left him some granola, and we set off again. There was one more mountain, Passaconaway, and an additional nine miles to go before we reached the chilled watermelon waiting in the cooler in our car.

It was a long day. Eighteen miles with thousands of feet of elevation gain over tough trails, without seeing another person the entire time. It was not the longest hike we'd ever taken, but it was the most grueling. Yet that night, as Atticus and I sat by the fire in the cabin we'd rented for the weekend, a deep peace fell upon me. I'd experienced tranquility in the mountains before. Plenty of it. But never quite like that night. It felt stronger, as if it was made to endure.

For the rest of the summer and coming fall, we continued to hike. We were getting ready for an absurd winter challenge, the entirety of which I was keeping to myself for the time being. Atticus and I were raising money for the Jimmy Fund and Dana-Farber Cancer Institute in memory of our late friend Vicki Pearson. We set out on an unlikely quest—to become the first man or dog ever to hike each of the forty-eight 4,000-footers twice in the ninety days of a single winter. Ninety-six peaks in ninety days.

In January of that winter, I decided we'd attempt to replicate that same journey through the Sandwich Range, only this time we reversed the route. We invited our Newburyport friend Tom Jones to join us. He was a good man, loyal and tough. He wasn't very experienced, but we'd taken him with us before and he understood that I always put Atticus first. He willingly accepted his role as our support for the day.

We left Tom's car where we had first entered the woods the summer before, and we drove to the Oliverian Brook Trail. Under dreary overcast skies on a morning raw and frozen, the trip up Mount Passaconaway seemed to take forever as we carefully made our way over icy, snow-covered rocks. Because of the conditions it took longer than expected to reach the summit. The good news was that the worst climb of the day was behind us. We proceeded to the summit of Whiteface and started out along the Kate Sleeper Trail. That's where our day changed.

Tom suggested we stop there and head down the Downes Brook Trail instead.

"You feeling okay?" I asked.

"Oh, yeah, I'm fine. Just worried about Atticus. That's all."

Atticus was fine, so I was surprised by his comment. Whatever the reason, Tom didn't want to continue on, and as much as this disappointed me, there is an unwritten rule that you can hike only as fast as the slowest member of your party, and you turn back when someone wants to. It didn't matter that Atticus and I were trying to set a record, and if we cut the hike short, we'd lose a day in a highly unpredictable season; you never knew when several feet of snow would block the trails for a week at a time. Nor did it matter that we'd have to return to do the Tripyramids on their own.

I gave Tom our options. "We can cut the hike short and descend the Downes Brook Trail, which hasn't been broken out all winter, through five miles of snow and across eleven stream crossings. Then add on another mile walking on the road. Or we head across the Sleepers for two and a half miles, on to the Tripyramids, which have been broken out by other hikers recently. The distance will be seven-point-nine miles. But most of it will be easier going."

I left the decision to Tom. He chose the Downes Brook Trail, thinking it would be a shortcut.

It was a horrible choice. The latest snowfall had not attached itself yet; it was powdery and deep. There was no firm footing, not even with our snowshoes on. We were up to our knees, and it went as high as our hips. Poor Atticus had to swim through it, often getting swallowed whole. Tom and I fell repeatedly. Under my breath, I cursed him. We stopped talking partly because of the dark thoughts in our heads, but also because of the exhausting descent. At a few of the stream crossings, the ice gave way and we had to be careful not to fall into the frigid waters. It took us much longer to get back down to the Kancamagus the shorter way. When we did, it was nine at night and five degrees and we still had a mile road walk back to my car. I was in a foul mood. I think we all were. But we did our best to hold it in.

However, something changed.

Here we were walking down the middle of a road in the White Mountains on an icy winter night with the dark silhouette of the pine trees and mountains surrounding us. In contrast, the glow of a huge moon was stunningly bright. There were no cars. It was quiet and otherworldly. Tom and I started talking again. We began to laugh again.

Ann Stampfer once told me, "It's the hikes where something goes wrong, where things don't turn out as expected, that are the most memorable."

Ann knew her mountains, and she was right. One of my favorite hiking memories is of that road walk. I can't fully explain why. Perhaps, even though we were falling short, I took curious pleasure in knowing that while we were cold and tired and had a way to go, everyone else we knew was home, safe, and warm. And many of them were bored.

We were on a quest, like those I only dreamed of until we started hiking. I could feel the frozen magnificence all around us. It was unalike the small city life Atticus and I had come to know. A life we'd soon give up.

Nine years have passed since that summer day on the Kate Sleeper Trailer, and we never made it back. There were always other places to explore, other summits to scale, and new challenges, Will being one of them.

I now accept that we will never go there again.

Still, the memory of that summer day comes to me often. It is so clear I can smell the pines along the ridge, feel the ferns on my calves, and remember the freedom of getting rid of my watch and Atticus's collar. At the best of times, thoughts of that trek are intoxicating. I smile as I think about a perfect summer day when the skies were blue, the trees were green, and we were both younger. It was the summer when I came to grasp that we'd become nemophilists and together we would always find our center in the forest.

When life is challenging and I find that I'm blocked by fear and the only way forward is through the darkness, I'm most hopeful when I remember what's important: simplicity. Simplicity in living, in loving, and in making our way through this world.

Of course it helps to be near the forest, or better yet in it. For the forest has always been with me, always called to me, even when I couldn't hear the message.

As I write this, Atticus is by my side. He's sleeping soundly. He now snores as loudly as Will used to. Looking at him, I think of the countless miles, all the mountains, and the memories. As we've grown older I now understand it's the trails we know well and remember fondly that comfort us, while the ones we've yet to take are those that force us to grow.

Life is different for us now that we no longer hike.

Peaceful, but different.

Yesterday afternoon, Aragorn was on our deck for the first time since last year, when Will was still alive. I baked a cherry pie and put it out on the railing to cool. Silly me. I hadn't seen any of the local bears for over a month, so I thought it was safe.

I was writing a letter to Ken and Ann when I looked up and saw him. He was ten feet away. His paws and claws were stained red with cherries. So was his muzzle.

I laughed at him.

"Enjoy it, Aragorn. It's not one of those crappy store-bought pies. I made it from scratch. And it's vegan!"

When I got up to get my camera he trotted down the stairs, and by the time we made it into the yard, he was in the high grass heading for the woods and the river beyond.

Atticus and I still stop at the little Dutch flower shop to get our flowers each week, even when money is tight. It's become a priority in my life. Some days I tell Carrie, "Whatever you have will do." But on other days, I ask for something more fragrant that Will would enjoy.

Atticus and I make the trip up to the Iron Mountain meadow from time to time. I sit looking up at Agiocochook and remember those last moments with Will. I say my prayers, giving thanks for that period in my life when I became more than what I had been. Before heading for home, I leave a single rose there for Will.

Last spring, I planted sweet williams at the edge of Wildflower Will's garden where the pumpkins used to be. I think it is my new favorite flower. But as Will taught me, any weed will do in a pinch. Because of him, when I spend time in the backyard I see things differently. I get down on my hands and knees to have the perspective he used to experience. I smell things and feel the grass beneath me. I sit in the places he used to stretch his body. When I mow the lawn I expect him to be dancing behind me like a drunken butterfly, with his mouth open and his eyes jolly.

Much like Marijane did, Ken and Ann Stampfer have become the family I always longed for, although time has caught up to us, for they no longer hike either. But we share a bond forged by the adventures we shared. Without Will, it's back to the way it used to be. But he still makes his way into every conversation. We are all better for having known him. (Okay, maybe not Atticus, but he was patient with Will, and was there for him when it mattered most.)

Rachael Kleidon has become a dear friend. She is as vital to us as ever now that Atticus is older. However, soon she will be busier. She's expecting. Rachael and her husband, Bryant, will be the best of parents. They've already decided on their daughter's name.

Sylvia. It means "from the forest."

As for me? I realize how blessed I am, to have known enchantment and understand the value of friendship and transformation. It is sometimes overwhelming for me to look back on my time with Will and consider everything that occurred. You would think that I feel pain at his passing, and loss for now living without him, but what exists within me is more enduring. For how am I to have lived those two and a half years with him and not feel the reverence for every bit of that time? I am proud to have been a part of his life, and honored to have been a witness to wonder.

I am fifty-four years of age. I'd like to think I have a long way to go before I too will be under the protective gaze of Agiocochook and Passaconaway. Whenever I get lost along the way from now on, I'll consider where I've come from, hold the forest and my memories close, and use a map left for me by an old friend. You see, I once knew a little white dog who taught me that old age is not a disease.

> Here is the world. Beautiful and terrible things
> will happen. Don't be afraid.
> —FREDERICK BUECHNER, *Beyond Words: Daily*
> *Readings in the ABC's of Faith*

Acknowledgments

On the way to completing this book, I took a wrong turn. I ended up in Memorial Hospital in North Conway, New Hampshire, for a few days, and followed that up with five weeks at Maine Medical Center in Portland, Maine. I'm told I nearly died. Several times. My kidneys shut down and I went on dialysis. My heart dropped to only 25 percent of its capability. I had pneumonia, blood clots, anemia, internal bleeding, a stroke, and septic shock. If it weren't for the numerous doctors, nurses, and technicians, I would not have finished *Will's Red Coat*. I wouldn't be here at all.

I would not have made it to the hospital in the first place if my friend Roy Prescott, the "morning voice of the Mount Washington Valley" and disc jockey at WMWV, hadn't saved my life by delivering me to the emergency room. Throughout my lengthy stay, he was there whenever he could be, bringing Atticus in for visits when the doctors bent the rules to allow it. I wouldn't have made it had it not been for the support of visiting friends. There are too many for me to name here. Having them by my side was the best medicine for my beleaguered heart.

Thankfully, *Will's Red Coat was* completed. My agent, Brian DeFiore, was there every step of the way. His support was outdone only by that of my incomparable editor at William Morrow, Cassie Jones, who was exceedingly patient while I was missing deadlines while trying to piece my life back together again. I am grateful for both. They are true professionals—and better people.

No story exists without a cast of individuals in the background. Laura Bachofner pointed Will in our direction. Without her, I wouldn't have known him. She is one of the two hundred and fifty thousand Facebook supporters we have on our Following Atticus page. Many a day, if I need inspiration, I look to their stories.

Additional gratitude goes to Christina and Mike Morse, Mary O'Hara, Wendy Anthony, Marybeth Cauffman, Donna Jean and J. C. Cassetta, Scott Ferrari and David Hallett, Ken and Ann Stampfer, Steve Smith, Ed Ryan, Claire Bigelow, Nancy Ryan, Peter Jason Riley, David Hall and Lisa Dorval, Romeo Dorval, Laini Shilitto, Jaime Jean Rogers, Megan Witt, Deb Brown, and Mark Hawthorne, for their kindness and their support of my goals and my writing.

Laura Cummings and her staff at White Birch Books see to it that personalized autographed and pawtographed copies of *Following Atticus* and *Will's Red Coat* are shipped all around the country and the world. Every author should be blessed with this kind of supportive indie bookstore to stand by them.

Rachael Kleidon is our veterinarian, and the most luminous soul I know. She was always there for Will and made concessions that allowed me to see him through to his final mountaintop in the way I envisioned. I wish that all of us could have a doctor this empathetic.

Although Will didn't come from the Conway Area Humane Society, I have a strong relationship with the staff and volunteers. However, no one is more special than the director, Virginia Moore. There are politics and personalities in every field, including animal rescue. Virginia restored my faith in the field with her selfless example.

Will's story would not be complete without the creative touch of Will's florist, Carrie Scribner, and her team at Dutch Bloemen Winkel, who always looked after Will's flowers: Orly White, Sheila Kackley, Tracy Vokey, Meg Hoffer, and Lizzy Duffy. Carrie is an artist at creating arrangements and made more than four hundred for my little friend. She is even better as a friend.

My late aunt, Marijane Ryan, played a significant role in my relationship with Will. Her love and experience in hospice were guiding lights for me to follow. She was a perfect example of how to walk in beauty, and what we shared will be with me for as long as I walk this earth. Annie Criscitiello offered moral support, witty correspondence, and laughter along the way. Sarah George is my favorite pen pal, and the sweetest witch I know. Lastly, there is Martha House, the "word thief" who brought my writing back to life while I was still recovering mine.